BULLDOG

EDITED BY
MALCOLM PRESLAND

ACKNOWLEDGEMENTS
The publishers would like to thank the following for help with photography: Malcolm Presland and
Melanie Vincent (Kofyn); Tony Darmanin (Sutus); Peter Davies (Kismond); Judith Daws (Outdoors);
Jenny Jones (Hijinks); Kelloe Bulldogs; Alan Walker; Bulldog Resue; Kevin Davis (Mystyle); Diddy Iking-Huber (Patdana);
Sara Lamont (Laroyal); Hearing Dogs for Deaf People; Pets As Therapy.

Cover photo: © Tracy Morgan Animal Photography (www.animalphotographer.co.uk)
Dog featured is Kofyn Kudja Wudja, owned and bred by Malcolm Presland and Melanie Vincent.

Page 2 © istockphoto.com/Justin Horrocks; page 10 © istockphoto.com/Serega
page 38 © istockphoto.com/Christine Gonsalves; page 41 © istockphoto.com/Peter Bokhorst
page 52 © istockphoto.com/Stephanie Phillips; page 61 © istockphoto.com/WilleeCole;
page 75 © istockphoto.com/iofoto; page 88 © istockphoto.com/Pavel Konovalov

The British Breed Standard reproduced in Chapter 7 is the copyright of the Kennel Club and published with the club's kind
permission. Extracts from the American Breed Standard are reproduced by kind permission of the American Kennel Club.

THE QUESTION OF GENDER
**The 'he' pronoun is used throughout this book instead of the rather impersonal 'it',
but no gender bias is intended.**

First published in 2010 by The Pet Book Publishing Company Limited
The Old Hen House, St Martin's Farm, Zeals, Warminster, BA12 6NZ, UK.
Reprinted in 2014

ISBN
978-1910488-08-9
1-1910488-08-9

Printed by Printworks Global Ltd. London & Hong Kong

CONTENTS

GETTING TO KNOW THE BULLDOG

The original fighting and baiting Bulldog was savage and ferocious – he needed to be – but to be a family pet, loyal companion and show dog, he had to be sweet-natured and trustworthy, and it is to the great credit of those early Bulldog breeders that they achieved this. The Bulldog's characteristics have come to represent the British temperament in that he conveys the impression of determination, strength and activity. He is alert, bold, loyal, dependable and courageous; he is fierce in appearance but possessed of an affectionate nature. In other words, he possesses the Bulldog spirit.

It comes as no surprise to learn that a Bulldog called Mr Hudson calmed panicking children and led them to safety, through thick, black smoke and flying debris, from the tower block next to the stricken World Trade Centre on September 11th 2001. Many famous politicians have associated themselves with the Bulldog, all wanting to be perceived as having his virtues of steadfastness and courage.

Over the years, he has been portrayed alongside the national hero, John Bull, in his Union Jack waistcoat and, indeed, he still is today. Winston Churchill, contrary to popular belief, never owned a Bulldog, preferring the company of Miniature Poodles. The Bulldog in America has become the mascot of numerous universities; he is the mascot of the American Marines, as well as having been made famous by the ubiquitous Bulldog emblem on Mack Trucks, which, in turn, are known for their strength and reliability.

COMPANION DOG

The Bulldog makes a wonderful pet and house dog. He loves human companionship and does not thrive as a lonely kennel dog. If you are thinking of keeping your Bulldog in a kennel, it is recommended that you have two for companionship. Despite his size – 55 lbs (25 kgs) for dogs, 50 lbs (23 kgs) for bitches – he does think he is a lap dog. His main ambition in life is to be on your bed or on the sofa, which should certainly not be encouraged, as we find that, as a puppy matures, this type of spoiling can lead to unwanted dominance. We all love our dogs, but it is not love to let a dog sit on your best chair or sleep on your bed; this will only lead to problems. While your Bulldog is still a pup, it must be clearly pointed out to him where his own bed is.

All Bulldogs love children, even if a dog has no prior knowledge of them. However, a young Bulldog is solid in stature and boisterous in nature and can easily knock a toddler over. Children must never be allowed to tease or provoke any dog, no matter how calm he appears, and a puppy must have his own space where he can relax in peace away from the kids.

A Bulldog is fairly easy to house train, although there are always exceptions, but we find that they tend to stand silently by a door asking to go out. If you miss this plea, he could have an 'accident' through no fault of his own.

Bulldog pups can be quite destructive during their teething stage and must be provided with large, indestructible toys and fresh marrowbones to enable them to exercise their teeth and jaws safely. Small balls, plastic toys and hide chews are not safe for a Bulldog's powerful jaws and could ultimately catch in his throat and choke him.

In my experience, I would suggest that the Bulldog is in every way desirable as a house dog and companion. He is a trustworthy playmate for children of all ages. Although his guarding abilities are somewhat dubious, if the local criminal fraternity are aware that a Bulldog is in residence, they will almost certainly give your home a wide berth, preferring easier pickings at a house with no dog in residence. However, if you want a dog that you can walk for miles in all winds and weathers and one which will unquestioningly do all that is asked of him, then the Bulldog is probably not for you.

A SUITABLE HOME

A Bulldog will quickly adapt to his new home whether it be a high-rise apartment or a country estate. Obviously, the latter would be preferred but, in reality, somewhere between the two is the norm. If the home is an apartment with no garden, then someone would need to be around most of the day to let the dog out to relieve himself at regular intervals. The other problem with an apartment, unless it is on the ground floor, is that most Bulldogs do not like going up stairs. One flight is fine, but more than one could prove difficult, especially in the dog's old age, which is something that should always be taken into account.

Ideally, the home should have a secure garden for the dog to explore. Remember to make sure of the security before bringing a new puppy home, as Bulldog pups are very inquisitive and will soon find a hole in a garden fence and be through it to explore new territories. Because of his friendliness to humans, your Bulldog could easily fall victim to dognappers – a crime that is sadly on the rise with the ever-increasing cost of puppies. Should you be unsure of your garden's security then never leave the dog alone if he cannot be seen at all times from the house.

This is a breed that has a natural affinity with children.

PHYSICAL CHARACTERISTICS

The general appearance of the Bulldog is that of a smooth-coated, thick-set dog, rather low in stature but broad, powerful and compact. The Bulldog has a short, smooth-textured coat and comes in a variety of colours, which should be brilliant and pure. These include: reds, fawns, brindles, white and also pied (a combination of white with any of the foregoing colours). Black, and black and tan, crop up in litters from time to time, but they are highly undesirable for the show ring. Occasionally, dogs will crop up with a Dudley nose (i.e. pink with no pigmentation), which also is a no-no. However, this does not mean that these dogs cannot make wonderful family pets. A few years ago, at Crufts, a lady showed me some photos of a litter of black and whites that she had just bred. I must say that they looked fabulous, and I am sure that they became great pets for their lucky owners. These colours are probably associated with the use of the Pug in some of the early crosses, which were used to bring down size and to improve temperaments.

I am often asked if the Bulldog tail is docked. The answer to this is: definitely not. Puppies are born with varying types of tail, from the correct 'pump handle' straight tail, to a short, screwed tail, which is not as desirable and requires a fair amount of work to keep free from dirt and infection.

The physical feature that sets the Bulldog apart from nearly all

BULLDOG COLOURS

Brindle.

Red.

White.

Fawn.

Pied.

other dogs is his 'tacked on' shoulder, which looks as if the dog's front legs have been stuck on his body. It is this feature that gives him his characteristic rolling gait when moving.

HEALTH ISSUES

Bulldogs are much maligned and unfairly criticised for their health problems, many of which could be avoided by good stock management. There are many misguided owners who obtain a Bulldog thinking they do not require any exercise. In reality, the more they are kept in fit, hard condition, the better.

The Bulldog Breed Council, together with many vets from all over the country, have developed a health test that they recommend should be passed annually by all dogs being used for breeding. This would mean that prospective puppy buyers would be able to see that their new pup's parents were in good health. But, as yet, the Kennel Club has not agreed to endorse puppy registration forms to the effect that the sire and dam have been health tested.

Over time, Bulldog breeders have slowly eradicated a lot of health problems that were always associated with the breed. This has been done with selective breeding by the stalwarts of the breed and still carries on today. All prospective matings should always be viewed with health issues, as well as conformation, high in priority as far as both sire and dam are concerned.

LIFE EXPECTANCY

I am often asked what age Bulldogs live to. Bulldogs, along with a great many other pedigree dogs, are not particularly long-lived, with the average age being around 10 years, although recently a friend of ours lost his much-loved dog at nearly 14.

Obviously, the needs of your Bulldog will change as he grows older, and it is important to give him special consideration in his later years so that he enjoys a good quality of life.

For information on caring for the older Bulldog, see Chapter Five: The Best of Care.

BULLDOG TEMPERAMENT

Some people may be intimidated by the physical appearance of the

Bulldog. They need not be, as Bulldogs are affectionate, gentle, good-natured, friendly and loyal dogs. The Breed Standard describes the Bulldog temperament as being: "Alert, bold, loyal, dependable, courageous, fierce in appearance but possessed of an affectionate nature". All of the above is generally correct to a greater or lesser degree, depending on the dog, as all dogs – even of the same breed – do differ to some extent. Let us look at the Breed Standard description in more detail:

- **Alert:** Well, we have had dogs who heard every movement and always let us know if there was anyone about, and we have had others who could sleep through door bells ringing and drunken revellers outside without so much as a raised ear!
- **Bold:** Generally, this is true of most Bullies. There are few things that frighten them apart from the occasional 'ghosty' that only they can see…
- **Loyal:** I always felt that all my dogs were stoically loyal until a very good friend of ours lost his much-loved pet Bulldog bitch. He was distraught over her loss and so we offered him a two-year-old bitch whom we had decided not to breed from. When he came to collect her, we were in tears, but we knew that this would be best for her, as a life spent on Paul's sofa would be much better than one spent in one of our kennels.

She obviously felt the same, as she got into his car and went off without a backward glance and went on to live to a ripe old age. She did come back to us on a couple of occasions when Paul went on holiday and was most put out having to live in a kennel again; she greeted Paul on his return like a demented thing – something that she never did to us.

- **Dependable:** This is certainly true of all the Bulldogs we have owned. They can be depended on always to do the unexpected. However, they can also be depended on to be fiercely protective of their family and are especially protective towards the children of the family.
- **Courageous:** Probably due to his ancestors' training in the pit and bull ring, the Bulldog is

certainly one of the most courageous of all animals. However, courage does not mean having a war-like spirit. On the contrary, today's Bulldog is usually anything but a fighter, although when aggrieved by another dog he can play his part to great credit to himself. He is, however, very long suffering and it usually takes a great deal of antagonism to arouse him.

- **Fierce in appearance but possessed of an affectionate nature:** This is the most accurate of descriptions. A Bulldog's appearance is, without doubt, fierce looking, as well as possessing a beautiful ugliness, as far as aficionados are concerned. His affectionate nature is always on show when around his family, with the children of the family being

You need to understand the Bulldog temperament in order to get the best from your dog.

11

particular favourites. He will be fiercely protective of them when called upon. In spite of their almost forbidding appearance, today's Bulldogs, are, in reality, one of the most docile and tractable dogs around. In the house no one could possibly desire a better, more faithful or trustworthy companion.

INSTINCTIVE BEHAVIOUR

The Bulldog was originally bred to bait bulls, and we have found that this instinct can still rear its ugly head occasionally. On one occasion we were walking our dogs along a path next to a field of young bullocks. An inquisitive bullock came over and put his nose through the fence to sniff at us as we went by. Vinnie, our 18-month-old prize stud dog, immediately grabbed hold of its nose and proceeded to try to pull the bullock through the fence. It was a case of the irristible force meeting the immovable object. Fortunately, we were able to remove said dog from the bullock with little or no harm being done to either, other than to both of their prides!

When near livestock, a Bulldog must be kept on a lead at all times. It goes without saying that when walking your dogs on any public footpath they should always be on a lead.

AFFINITY WITH CHILDREN

All of the bull breeds – and especially the Bulldog – have a strong affinity with children. It always surprises me when I am

The Bulldog is loyal and loving, and can be protective of his family.

out with a Bulldog to find how attracted children are towards him, particularly bearing in mind his apparently ferocious outward appearance. Often the parents will chastise their child for wanting to stroke the Bulldog, probably worrying that the child may get bitten. Obviously the dog's owner should always be asked first, but, in the vast majority of cases, the dog will like nothing better than a hug from a child.

When a Bulldog puppy is brought into a home, the children need to be taught not to constantly bother the pup and pick him up. A young Bulldog pup who is dropped by a young child could easily receive life-threatening injuries. The new pup should always be given a sleeping area of his own where he can

retreat when he is tired or when the children are getting a little too exuberant. The children should always be taught that when the pup is there, he should be left alone. If necessary, the use of a crate can ensure that the puppy has an undisturbed rest. A puppy will soon learn that his crate is a place of peace and harmony that he can go to whenever he feels the need.

Children must also be taught never to smack the puppy. The puppy should know his place in the household pecking order, but a firm "No" when he is misbehaving is all that is required. The adults of the family should undertake the pup's main training with the children taking a back seat. Never allow children to play too roughly with the pup, as this could encourage aggressive behaviour. This may be controllable in a young pup but will certainly foster problems when that pup becomes a fully mature 55-lb (25-kg) adult.

When out and about with your Bulldog, children should never be left in sole charge of the dog. Bulldogs are expensive to buy, and they are currently being stolen in quite high numbers. For this reason, children should always be accompanied by an adult when outside the confines of the home. Another thing to bear in mind is that a fully mature Bulldog is a very powerful animal, who could easily drag a child to the ground if he spots something that takes his fancy – and if this should be on the other side of a busy main road, disaster could easily ensue.

Of course, all of this is pretty much common sense, and, if reared and looked after sensibly, dog, children and adults should become firm friends and companions for many years.

LIVING WITH OTHER ANIMALS

I am often asked how a Bulldog would get on with other family pets, be they dogs or cats. In my experience, as long as the newcomer is introduced carefully to the resident dogs, there are rarely any problems. If the newcomer is a puppy, make sure that he does not bother the older dogs to the point of retaliation. Always remember that the puppy's milk teeth are as sharp as needles and can inflict great pain, even though he may be only playing. Having said that, the resident dogs should be allowed to show the newcomer who is the boss and most will do so early on in their relationship.

For this reason a puppy and adult should never be left alone until you are sure they are going to get on. Personally, we never leave any of our dogs together when we are not there. Trouble can break out over the most trivial of things, and we have found that even the most convivial of dogs who have been brought up together can fall out occasionally. If you are not around to call a halt to proceedings, you could come home to something resembling the Somme!

We have always had a cat or two in residence wherever we have lived, and I suppose we have been lucky that, in the most part, they have been long suffering where the dogs – and especially the puppies – are concerned. Again, if the puppy is introduced at an early age, there should be little or no trouble.

TRAINABILITY

It is often thought that Bulldogs are not very intelligent. This could not be further from the truth. The Bulldog is very intelligent; it is just that he would rather be cuddled than learn a new trick. He can, however, be rather lazy and extremely stubborn. It is at these times that a Bulldog's intelligence comes to the fore. He can nearly always get this own way, usually by giving you his special 'sad' look, which, in turn, has the desired effect of making you feel guilty – and bingo! – you cave in to his wants. The facial wrinkles give a Bulldog the most expressive face, and one that always lets you know what he is thinking or what kind of mood he is in.

Despite being regarded as a stubborn breed – and it is this quality that seems to attract many people to the Bulldog – they can be trained for obedience, agility and other disciplines, such as carting or heelwork to music. Although they may not attain Olympic-style heights, they can still reach quite a high standard. The Bulldog has a pretty laidback attitude to everything he does, which makes him an ideal companion to have around the

Generally, the Bulldog is tolerant of other animals and will live happily alongside other pets.

Loving and affectionate by nature, the Bulldog makes a perfect therapy dog.

THERAPY DOGS

Because of the Bulldog's conformation, he is not naturally suited to work as an assistance dog. He is, however, ideally suited to the role of therapy or PAT (Pets as Therapy) dog. Therapy dogs provide a special service to local communities by going into homes for the elderly, hospitals, hospices and special-needs schools where the residents, patients and students find the company of a dog to be most rewarding. It is also a most satisfying pastime for the handler. The Bulldog's laid-back attitude to life, coupled with his naturally affectionate nature and love of human companionship, makes him perfect for this role.

An older dog would nearly always be preferable, as a boisterous young dog could accidentally hurt an elderly person by jumping up at them. All dogs are given a thorough assessment to ensure their temperaments are 100 per cent sound before starting working as therapy dogs.

SUMMING UP

The fact that you are reading this book must mean that you have recently acquired a Bulldog or are about to, so you should be congratulated for choosing what I consider to be the perfect family pet. I hope that this introduction has given you an insight into our wonderful and special breed. You will find him to be a true and loyal companion, and, once owned

house. The pleasure of having a well-behaved family pet is immense. This is not to say that they do not make good guards, as most Bulldogs will fiercely protect those that they love.

We had a Bulldog bitch who disliked the show ring immensely. However, we felt that she was an exceptional specimen, so we thought we would train her at our local obedience class to get her more amenable to showing. The down-stay was a little difficult for her, as she would always want to sit rather than lie down. She loved the retrieve part of the exercises to such a degree that she thought she should retrieve all the other dogs' dumbbells as well, which did cause a bit of a furore. We did get her to quite a high standard in obedience, but, sadly, she never

enjoyed the show ring so we stopped showing her. There is really no point in dragging a dog along to a dog show when – even if they are a very good specimen of the breed – they clearly do not enjoy it.

Local training and show classes that use the reward system should be attended, if possible, as soon as the puppy is fully vaccinated. Show dogs have their own training system known as ring craft, where you and your dog can be taught the basics of showing and get all the information needed to enter shows. You will probably find that your vet has the phone numbers for either obedience or ring craft clubs in your area. Your new puppy's breeder should also help you with regard to the various canine activities.

Once you have owned a Bulldog, no other breed will do.

by a Bulldog, your life will never be quite the same.

The Bulldog is a dog of great character and individuality; he loves his family with a passion. He will make you laugh with his antics and comfort you when you are down. He needs to be part of family life and is not suited to long, lonely periods on his own. He enjoys either lounging in front of the fire, fetching a ball, or allowing the kids to dress him up – and he will not hesitate to protect you from the 'ghostie' in the kitchen. He will defend his territory with stoic determination and, if necessary, use his sour expression to ward off evil.

In return, you must keep him in fit, clean condition and give him love and respect. Once you have been owned by the unique, quaintly British character that is the Bulldog, you will never want to be without one – promise!

THE FIRST BULLDOGS

Chapter 2

It is generally accepted by dog historians that, in the far distant mists of time, mankind and a wolf-like creature befriended one another. This animal was the progenitor of today's dogs, and all the breeds have since evolved through selective breeding.

Researchers generally agree, although difficult to prove, that the Bulldog traces its origins to the fierce Molossian dogs of Epirus, which was part of ancient Greece. The Molossi were a Greek people, who claimed descent from Molossus, a grandson of Achilles, and are said to have emigrated from Thessaly into Epirus. Their Molossian hounds were celebrated in antiquity and were much prized for hunting. There are Assyrian bas-reliefs depicting this ancient breed with compact bodies and short faces, which can now be seen in the British Museum.

These 'hounds' were traded throughout the Mediterranean and it is believed that Phoenician traders introduced them to England around 600 years BC.

BRITISH ROOTS

In his book, *Researches into The History of the British Dog*, in 1866, George R. Jesse states that by the time the Romans came to Britain these dogs had been bred by the inhabitants as guard and war dogs; they excelled at combats in the arena and in pursuits of the chase. The Roman Claudian described them as the "broad-mouthed dog of Britain". Strabo, a contemporary of Julius Ceasar, said of Britain in 63-64BC: "It produces corn, cattle, gold, silver, and iron, which also forms its exports together with skins, slaves, and dogs of a superior breed for the chase. The Gauls use these dogs in war, as well as others of their own breed."

Gratius Faliscus, in AD8, describe them as the "Pugnaces of Britain" and in his hunting poem he writes:

"But if you visit the Morinian shores,
Whose ebbing waves oft leave the ocean doubtful,
And thence cross o'er to Britain, set aside
The form and colour, which in British dogs
Are the worst points, but, when the tug of war
And inbred courage spur them to their work,
Then is their metal seen: Molossian hound
In vain competes with them."

These authors relate that by the time the Romans came to these shores, the dogs bred in Britain were redoubtable animals, highly prized and superior to those in Epirus. There can be little doubt

Dogue of Burgos, typical of the war dogs taken from Britain to other parts of the Roman empire.

that they were exported by the Romans to all parts of their empire for the sports of the amphitheatre. It must be assumed that not all of these animals were killed in the arena; it is likely that breeding pairs were kept to assure a supply of locally bred animals for the sport.

At that time, Britain possessed at least three species of dogs: the formidable, large mastiff type described by Gratius, the scenting hound described by Oppian, and the Greyhound referred to by Nemesianus. Jesse's thorough research of the archives points out that the dog was also highly esteemed among the Celts. Aneurin, a Celtic poet of the 6th century, describes the battle of Cattraeth, where his countrymen were defeated by the Saxons. A north British chieftain says, when deploring the loss of his companions:

" There escaped only three from the power of their swords,
Two War Dogs from Aeron and Cynon,
And I."

HUNTING AND GUARDING

Saxon herdsmen who reared and guarded the great droves of swine, which ranged the vast forests of beech and oak, must have kept many fierce dogs to assist them and to protect their charges from the attacks of wolves and marauders. The chief recreation of the Saxons was hunting, and their dogs were considered very valuable and bred with care. Every nobleman or great landowner had his hund-wealh or dog keeper.

The Anglo Saxon kings established the first rules of the hunt; these were followed by game laws enacted at a Parliament in 1016 by the Danish King Cnut (Canute). In addition to the ecclesiastical and secular laws, he instigated the "Constitutiones de Foresta" or forest laws and decreed death for anyone caught hunting in Crown Domains, other than those who had the King's permission. These laws were added to by William The Conqueror (1066-1087) and enforced by his successors.

Every man dwelling within any forest might keep a "mastiff" about his house for the defence of it and his goods, only if it was lawfully maimed, lawed (chopping off three toes, thus making them lame and unable to run). This practice continued throughout the reigns of

Elizabeth 1 (1558-1603) and James (1603-1625). John Manwood, author of *A Brefe Collection of the Lawes of the Forrest, 1598*, was a barrister of Lincoln Inn and gamekeeper of Waltham Forest as well as holding other appointments under the Queen. Writing at that time, he states:

"Budaeus calleth a Mastive Molossus; in the old British speech they doe call him a Masethefe, and by that name they doe call all manner of Barking curres, that doe use to Barke about mens houses in the night, because that they doe Mase and feare away theeves from houses of their masters"

BULL-BAITING

'Mastiffs' was a term applied to a group of general-purpose dogs, other than hounds, spaniels or toy dogs. Some within that group were used from a very early period for bear and bull-baiting. It is written that in the time of King Edward the Confessor prior to 1066, the city of Norwich paid £20 to the King and £10 to the Earl, and beside these payments: 21 shillings and four pence for measure of provender, six sextaries of honey, a bear and six bear dogs, "et 1. Ursum et VI. Canes ad ursum" (*Ellis's Introduction to the* Domesday Book, vol. 1 p. 206).

Legend has it that, around 1209, Earl Warren, Lord of Stamford, witnessed an enraged bull being tormented by a pack of dogs. He was so delighted, that he donated a field to the

Bull baiting was popular for many centuries, and dogs were bred specifically for the sport.

local butcher on the understanding that they supplied a bull to be baited by trained dogs every November. This 'sport' became so fashionable that by the end of the 13th century, most market towns in Britain had a bull ring.

In the 14th century, Geoffrey Chaucer's Knight's Tale from *The Canterbury Tales*, vividly describes a fierce and extinct breed of dog called Alaunt – this name was variously written as Alan, Alande, Alant, Alaune, Alaunus, Alaunt, and Allan. Strength, speed and ferocity were among the attributes of the Alaunt. His dangerous nature, even occasionally directed towards his owner, is noted by Edmund de Langley, Second Duke of York between 1406-1413. In *Master of the Game*, he describes him as a short-headed dog, pugnacious and gifted, with an inclination to

hang on to anything he attacked. He is said to have combined the qualities of the Greyhound and those of the Mastiff, Alano, which was a Spanish name for a Mastiff breed of dog. The Alaunt seems to have been the original war dog and is described in Cotgrave's French-English dictionary published in 1632 as follows:

Allan: a big, strong thicke-headed and short-snowted dog; the brood whereof came first from Epirus.
Allan de Boucherie: is like our mastive, and serves butchers to bring in fierce oxen and to keep their salls.
Allan gentil: is like a greyhound in all properties and parts, his thicke and short head excepted.
Allan vautre: a great and ugly curre of that kind (having a big head, hanging lips,and slowching eares) kept onely to bait the Beare and wild Boare.

In his book, *Researches into The History of the British Dog,* Jesse states that Prestwick Eaton wrote from San Sebastian in Spain to George Wellingham, in St. Swithen's Lane, London, in 1631and 1632, for several things, amongst which he wanted: "a good mastive dogge", his case of bottles "replenyshed with the best lickour," and "pray," said he, "procuer mee two good Bulldoggs and let them bee sent by y first ship."

This was the first reference in English to the Bulldog in writing, and we must therefore conclude that, by that time, the Mastiff and the Bulldog had become two distinct breeds. The latter obviously deriving his name from the sport of bull baiting

Baiting, at first, was conducted with large dogs which attempted to bring the bull down by taking hold of the ear, and it would be

The sport of bear baiting was often used as a royal spectacle, to entertain foreign visitors.

most probable this dog was the Alaunt, the common ancestor of the Mastiff and the Bulldog, which had so impressed the Romans. But, in time, it was discovered that a smaller dog who flew at the bull's head to grab his nose or any other part of the face, in powerful jaws, could just as easily bring a bull down and pin it. So fanciers selected smaller but formidable, courageous specimens capable of carrying out these requirements.

In his book, *The Dog*, written 1872, Idstone describes how, in 1680, it was said of the breed that, though small and low, when once they seized the throat "you might sooner cut them in pieces than make them let go their hold". They were frequently killed – "the bull taking them on his horns, and tossing them up in the air like footballs."

Idstone goes on: "He is described by Bewick" (a famous wood engraver and author of *A General History of Quadrupeds, 1790*, as: "low in stature but strong and muscular and probably the most courageous creature in the world; with a short nose, a projecting underjaw, and always fastening about the lip, the tongue, the eye, or some part of the face, and hanging there in spite of every effort of the bull to disengage himself."

ROYAL PATRONAGE

The sport of bull and bear-baiting continued for centuries under royal patronage. Indeed, Queen Elizabeth 1 is said to have often entertained visiting foreign dignitaries and ambassadors to such spectacles. It is from this period onwards that much was written on Mastiffs and Bulldogs.

Stow, writing in 1572, stated that the most famous pits appeared in 1565-66 at certain playhouses in London, The Globe, The Swan, The Rose and Hope, on the South Bank of the Thames, being the most popular. A German traveller and author, Hentzner, writes in his *Itinerary* in 1598 that: "…the bulls and bears are fastened behind and then worried by great English Bull-dogs" (translation from the German) and carries on with gory descriptions of the spectacle provided.

Wasp, Child and Billy. Detail from a hand-coloured engraving, after a painting by H.B. Chalon. London, 15 May 1809.

Idstone says that by 1824, as interest in the 'sport' waned, the breed was said to be degenerating, although specimens of a coarse but courageous sort had been in the hands of prize-fighters and coachmen for some 50 years. He states that many of these early specimens were disfigured by cropping, and sometimes they were found with their ears shaven off completely.

BATTLE TO SAVE THE BULLDOG

With Queen Anne's accession to the throne in 1702, the 'sport' no longer had royal patronage and was only frequented by the poorer sections of the population. In 1835, the Humane Act of Parliament abolished the baiting of bulls and bears and dog fighting in public. The sporting fraternity of the time then turned to illicit dog fighting and Bulldogs were specially trained for this pastime.

However, although some fanciers relied on the pure breed, in time, others crossed their dogs with terriers to obtain a faster turn of speed and so get the first hold. The Bull Terrier was born and soon replaced the Bulldog as a fighting dog.

The Bulldog now faced extinction, but diehard fanciers decided that a breed that was so distinctively British and that had existed in these lands for centuries should be saved. In his book, *The Bulldog, A Monograph*, published in 1899, Edgar Farman states that by 1840 very few thoroughbred examples existed, although some specimens could be obtained in London, Birmingham and Sheffield.

In 1859 the first dog show was held; Bulldog classes were offered at the Birmingham show of 1860. The fancy now had an incentive to perpetuate the breed. In 1864, a few enthusiasts met to form the first Bulldog Club, and although their aims were admirable, it lasted only three short years. A new group of fanciers met in 1874 at the Blue Post public house Newman Street, London, to form The Bulldog Club. Their intent was to save the breed from gradual extinction, and from being crossbred to what they considered to be imported

Early 18th century Bulldog.

I8th century Bulldogs.

Spanish milk-cart dogs. In 1875 the current Bulldog Club was established with a framework of rules and a written description of the Bulldog, which was later adopted as the Breed Standard.

James Watson, an American, writing in 1905, recalls visiting England with his father in 1877 to 1880. They had previously visited in 1868 when they had gone to Bill George's Bulldog kennels. During the later visit, Watson recalls meeting Alfred George – Bill George's son – at the Alexandra Palace dog show. When looking at the Bulldogs, they commented on seeing an alteration in them since their last visit. Alfred's reply was: "Oh, there has been a great change since you went away. You will see some of the old sort at father's, but they don't do for showing."

THE FIRST CHAMPION

The first Bulldog Champion was Ch. Old King Dick, owned by Jacob Lamphier of Sheffield. He was a red smut dog of 48 lbs (22 kgs), winning his title in 1865 at the Birmingham Show. He lived to be eight years old and figured prominently in the pedigree of many dogs of the time. Henry Webb, writing in 1872 and assisted by Frank Adcock, a Bulldog specialist, who later tried to import large Spanish Bulldogs to cross with the indigenous specimens of the day, says that Old King Dick was exhibited at various dog shows in London and the provinces between 1861 and 1865. He was a universal favourite with the judges, winning no less than 16 prizes.

The manner of his death clearly exemplifies the affectionate disposition, the fidelity and attachment of a breed of dog too often considered to possess a ferocious and unfeeling nature. His owner, Jacob Lamphier, a well-known breeder of the species, was afflicted with consumption, and at intervals, during the last 12 months of his life, was confined to his room. Old King Dick, being a great favourite, was his constant companion. In April 1866, Jacob Lamphier died. Dick was at the time confined to the yard and continued to be so until after the funeral. The first day he was let loose, he rushed upstairs into his master's room, and made straight for the easy chair in which his master used to sit. He found it was vacant, so he put his paw on the bed, looked under it, and rushed backwards and forwards, crying piteously. He ran to a back room, which he searched thoroughly, before returning to the bedroom.

Miss Lamphier, Jacob's daughter, who was in the room, tried to comfort him, but without success. He lay himself down on

22

the rug before the fire and never seemed to lift his head up again. No caress, no endearments could rouse him. He refused all food that was offered him. He gradually fell away from the fat, heavy dog that he had been to a mere skeleton, and on the fourth day after he had missed his old master, King Dick died.

SIGNIFICANT BULLDOGS

Jacob Lamphier owned a number of Bulldogs, including Venom, Meg, Madge, Romanie, and Adam – the first Bulldog to be registered in the Kennel Club Stud book.

One of Ch. King Dick's descendants was Ch. Crib, also known as Sheffield Crib, who was bred by Jacob Lamphier's son. He was a 64-lb (29-kg) brindle-and-white dog, born in 1871, and who died unbeaten. This dog was a prolific sire with a massive influence on the breed. At the Bulldog Club shows held in 1892 and 1893, he figured in the pedigree of every dog entered and was responsible for establishing four of the old main strains of the breed.

Watson recalls that the good dogs of the day between 1877 and 1882 were: Sir Anthony, Gambler, Doon Brae, Slenderman, Smasher, King Cole, Sancho Panza, Venom (Layton's), Rosy Cross (George Raper's best

Ch. Old King Dick: The first Bulldog Champion.

bitch, for he was then a prominent Bulldog man), Hartley's Venom, Roselle, Faust, Lord Nelson, Richard Coeur De Lion (Raper's), and then, best of all, came Monarch.

It is impossible in a book of this size to list the names of breeders of distinction and the top dogs of the time, but the ardent student of the breed will be pleased to know that a wealth of information may be obtained from Jackson and Bowers' *Bulldog Pedigrees (1892, 1894, 1898)*, which is a list of all known Bulldogs and their reputed ancestors in three volumes followed by *British Bulldogs 1909* by Mary Thomas, which continues the work done by Jackson and Bowers, covering the period 1897 to 1901 and listing 3,500 names.

It was said at the time that a Bulldog, Ch. King Orry, born in 1889, a son of Pagan (a Ch. Gamester grandson), was noted for the prevalence of dogs possessing long skulls with excellent layback, nice turn of underjaw, neat ears and shapely bodies.

GROWING POPULARITY

As Bulldogs became more popular and the show scene became established not only in Britain but also in America, top dogs were sold for big sums of money. It was the practice of the time to indicate a price for exhibits in show catalogues. Some of these were grossly inflated by owners, who had no intention of selling their dogs, but would be tempted to do so if offered the price indicated.

The catalogue for the Bulldog Club Championship Show of 1892, compiled by Frank Crowther, is truly a work of art in book form of parchment and vellum, listing by name the officers, committee members and names and addresses of members of the club who came not only from all over Britain, but also from Dublin, Canada and the USA. The Breed Standard of the time was published, and, in alphabetical order, the 137 Bulldogs entered. Each dog is found in class order, with a three-generation pedigree and a sale price. A list of names and addresses of exhibitors is also included. There are reports of the Bulldog Club for 1890, 1891 and 1892, and reporter's notes from the following dog publications of the day: *Stock Keeper, British Fancier, Fancier's Gazette* and *The Field*. These are followed by stud dog adverts with highly priced stud fees:

*His Lordship (Winner of over 50 First and special prizes) at £4:4:0
Stilletto (Winner of 13 First and other prizes) at £3:3:0.
Ch. Forceps £5:5:0 (prepaid)
Ch. Datholite £5:5:0 (prepaid)
British Pedro £2:2:0
Don Salano £3:3:0
Don Carlos £2:2:0.*

*The winner of the Challenge Class on that occasion was: Bedgebury Lion (male), stud book number 27555, sire: The Alderman 13021, dam: Lydia, date of birth 16/8/1888, breeder exhibitor Mr P. B. Beresford-Hope whose dog was not for sale.
2nd His Lordship 29741, sale price £350.
3rd Ch. British Monarch 19543, sale price £2,500.*

BREEDING TO THE STANDARD
In his book, *Show Bulldogs*, published by *Our Dogs* in 1904,

The Lamp Tavern, Birmingham in the 1880s showing owners with their Bulldogs.

Sidney Deacon includes pictures of 22 Champions, which clearly demonstrate that breeders had, in a very short space of time, bred specimens as close as possible to the Breed Standard of the time.

Ch. Baron Sedgemere was sold by his owner Sam Woodiwiss for £600 in 1900 – no mean sum in those days. The following year, 1901, Int. Ch. Rodney Stone, owned by Mr Walter Jeffries, was sold to Mr R. Croker of New York for the huge sum of £1,000, which caused a sensation in the dog world at that time.

Several dogs were sold to the USA for similar prices up to 1904 when Deacon's book was published. The most notable bitch born at the turn of the century was Ch. Roseville Blaze, owned by Mr. G. Woolons. She was regarded by the top breeders and judges of the time to be the Standard personified. Unfortunately, she was barren.

Writing in 1905, H. St. John

Cooper states that there was a considerable difference in appearance between the current Bulldog and his ancestor of 100 years ago. The prominent dogs of the day were descendants of King Orry – Ch. Prince Albert was a 43-lb (19.5-kg) brindle, and was described as having "great bone, beautiful turn of forearm and a head chockfull of type." He was owned by Luke Crabtree and won over 400 first and special prizes, and he also sired many winners of the day. Other top dogs were: Moston Major, Prince of Darkness, Mersey King, Carthusian Cerberus, bred by Cyril Jackson, Ch. Nuthurst Doctor, Justice of the Peace, Berner's Ingoldsby Lawyer, Ch. Boomerang, Ch. Broadlea Squire, St. Amant, Kilburn King, Ivel Daedalus, His Nibs, Bob Upanwyn, Probang and Am. Ch. Rodney Smasher.

According to A.G. Sturgeon, writing in 1919, the highlight was seeing an entry of 514 dogs and bitches gathered at the London Bulldog Society Show of 1909. He praises Prince Albert for also producing many winning descendants. He writes: "One of the best bitches (and it is extremely doubtful if there ever was a better) is Ch. Oak Nana, by Oak Leaf by Solid Oak, bred

SIGNIFICANT BULLDOGS

Ch. British Monarch: His listed sale price was £2,300 in 1892.

Int. Ch. Rodney Stone: Sold to the US for big money.

Ch. Roseville Blaze: This bitch was regarded as being the Breed Standard personified.

Ch. Keysoe Golden Sovereign: In the 1930s, the modern type of Bulldog emerged.

Ch. Pugilist: A top winning dog of his time. He was also used as a patriotic emblem by the Press during the Second World War.

from a bitch (his own) without the slightest pretensions to show form. But the winning blood was there, and for generations, on both sire and dam's side."

Old George Mortimer, a renowned dog man in America, said that Ch. Oak Nana was the best model, dog or bitch, ever exported to the USA – "and the States has had the best from this country for the last twenty years."

THE MODERN DOG

Bulldogs were beginning to look like the modern dog, and this is confirmed by the photographs in A.G. Sturgeon's book of 1924, showing Tweedside Red Squire, Wardley Monarch, Ashford Minerva, Irish Alaunt, Ch. Hefty Son O' Mike, Ch. Jutland Jupiter, Wenden Citizen, Ch. Roscow Dobbie, Ch. Sweet September, Irish Challenger, Ch. Oak Nana and Oak Leaf.

By 1932, winning dogs could just as easily have been exhibited to full honours at the turn of the 21st century. These included, to name a few: Barnard Green I've Arrived (B), Ch. Rolls Rose (B), Ch. Dame' Double (B), Ch. Glendene Sun-Ya Ch. Keysoe Golden Sovereign, Ch. Pugilist. Dunstonian Dignity, Ch. Crewe So Solarium, Jasperdin of Din and Ch. Basford Revival.

Some prominent kennel names

of the time were: Allithorne, Basford, Din, Falstone, Glendene, Leodride, Roseville, Tottonian, and Vindex. It is interesting to note that stud fees at that time had remained at 2 to 3 guineas. Kennel Club registrations for the breed were 853 in 1900, but by 1908 the breed had become so popular that they reached their peak at 1,739.

THE BREED IN DECLINE

By 1918 the breed was in serious decline with only 360 registrations. In the last 14 months of the First World War, practically no puppies were bred, as a special licence to breed had to be obtained from the Kennel Club, and these were almost impossible to obtain.

Post-war registrations hovered between 1,000-1,500, until the outbreak of the Second World War, at which point there was a dramatic decline in numbers down to 270 registrations in 1941.

A monthly Bulldog magazine was started in May 1946 and continued on and off as a quarterly until The Bulldog Club Incorporated began to publish its own publication in December 1965.

THE STORY OF INT. CH. BOSWORTH QUEEN

No history of the Bulldog would be complete without the story of International Champion Bosworth Queen. Born in 1937, she was bred by Mr J.S Duncan and purchased by Jimmy Knode. He was a popular bookmaker who travelled 3,000 miles by land, sea and air inside 18 months, and won £3,000 worth of trophies. In June 1939, Ch. Bosworth Queen appeared in a diamond and platinum collar, which caused a sensation. By 1940 she had amassed 13 English Championships and an Irish title.

Once the war started, Queenie was used as a fundraiser at rallies and exhibitions, and collected £100,000 for various charities. At Trafalgar Square alone, she collected more than £40,000 for a Lancaster bomber. During this period, it is said that over a million people saw and tickled her, so much so that the hair under her chin completely disappeared! Her owner, James Knode, refused an American offer of £3,000 for his beloved Queenie.

Ch. Bosworth Queen: A leading show dog and a famous fundraiser.

Ch. Noways Chuckles: The breed's one and only Crufts Best in Show winner, 1952.

Ch. Outdoors Country Gent and his daughter Ch. Kentee Kizzy at Outdoors made Bulldog history by being the first dog and bitch to win Bulldog of the Year from the same kennel.

Photo: Sally Ann Thompson.

POST-WAR REVIVAL

Although entire kennels were lost during the course of the war, some good ones survived, and a number that started soon after the war came to an end now came into their own. These included: Allithorne, Coventrian, Crossbank, Dunvegan, Eastgate, Grenville, Maelor, Maythorpe, Morovian, Of Wiggin, and Noways, all of which dominated the breed well into the 1960s. In fact, the only Bulldog ever to win Best in Show at Crufts, in 1952, was Ch. Noways Chuckles born on 17 October 1950, sired by Ch. Prince of Woodgate out of Noways Victoria, bred and owned by John Barnard.

During the 1950s more famous kennels made their presence felt: Kippax, Beechlyn,

Broadford, Of The Regions, followed by Baytor, Blytholme, Broomwick, Bryneatons, Crosroads, Jackath, Mellea, Moselian, Outdoors, Petworth, Qualco, Quintic, Sevenup, Thydeal, Tuffnuts and Walvra, all of whom bred top dogs. In fact, Outdoors Bulldogs are shown with success to this day.

A NEW ERA

The 1960s saw the emergence of new kennels and the ones that began to make their presence felt were: Aldridge, Atomstone, Atozed, Castizo, Daneham, Denborough, Eskaidee, Hawkshope, Merriveen, Ocobo, Petworth, Setsquare, Tretun, and Wedgebury.

Then, from the 1970s to the 1990s: Belushi, Britishpride,

Bondabull, Bonifacio, Brandywell, Brampton, Cabinteely, Chappark, Coatesmar, Culverhay, Dawnstar, Esclusham, Foresquare, Gwenstan, Hobtop, Iceglint, Isgraig, Jumano, Kanchee, Kelloe, Kingrock, Kofyn, Leydud, Linmist, Lynmans, Mystyle, Nobozz, Packapunch, Ringablok, Sutus, Wencar and Wyecaple – many of which are active today.

Some names that have come to the fore more recently are: Biddle, Bollglade, Bullpei, Jaminic, La-Royal, Mellafella, Mellowmood, Sealaville and Terlingfair.

The Bulldog Club Incorporated provides a comprehensive magazine twice yearly and has done so since 1965. This is a great source of information and

Ch. Mystyle Eye Candy Ocobo: A current top winning Bulldog.

has always contained photographs and adverts of all winning dogs. The student of the breed may be lucky to obtain older copies available for sale from time to time through internet auction sites.

THE BULLDOG IN THE USA

Although it was claimed in the 19th century that the Bulldog did not fare well outside these shores, the truth is that Bulldogs flourish well when properly looked after.

There is no doubt that some of the early settlers to the New World took their Bulldogs with them, and there is a wealth of anecdotes in North American literature about their exploits. Watson, author of *The Dog Book 1905*, a comprehensive book on all breeds, says that the first presentable Bulldog shown in the USA was a lightweight called Donald, sent over by the Irish exhibitor Sir William Verner for the New York show of 1880. In 1881, Mr Mason showed Noble, a dog that had done some winning in England, who beat Mr J.P. Barnard's dog, Bonnie Boy, a son of the English dog, Slenderman. Although several more dogs were imported from England, it was only when Col. John E. Thayer (first president of the Bulldog Club of America) bought Blister, and Robinson Crusoe from George Raper, and Britomartis from Ron S. Barlow that the best Bulldogs were seen in the United States.

In 1890, the Bulldog Club of America (BCA) was formed. By 1893, Bulldog entries had increased 50 per cent over the previous year and the breed became firmly established. Early owners and exhibitors who competed against each other included Mr J.B. Vandergrift with a King Orry son, Ch. Katerfelto, who was said to be better than his sire, and Mr R. Croker Jnr. campaigned Persimmon,

Ch. Bromley Crib: A British import to the US.

RECORDING HISTORY

Enno Mayer, a renowned artist, sculptor, anatomist and dog breeder, published his book, *The Bulldog*, in 1948, which provides a comprehensive history of the Bulldog in America up to that date, with reprints of the book in 1952 and 1960. Col. Bailey C. Hanes, an enthusiast well acquainted with some of the top Bulldoggers in Britain, began to collect material in 1948 for his book, *The New Complete Bulldog*, published in 1956, and reprinted and updated six times until 1987, which similarly and comprehensively traces the development of the breed in the USA.

although this was a struggle, as the dog was pining on arrival from England and would not eat. Both these gentlemen built up their kennel with imported English dogs. Vandergrift imported Ch. Portland, Ch. Housewife, Ch. Lady Dockleaf, Meersham Jock, Fascination, Lark-Hill Agrippina, Duke of Albermarle, Chester Monarch and others, making his kennel one of the most outstanding of the time.

Trenor L. Park, founding Vice President of the BCA, imported the famous Ch. Bedgebury Lion. James Mortimor imported the famous Ch. King Orry for

Colonel Hilton in 1893, who transmitted his great head qualities to the breed in America. Mr Lawson paid $6,000 for a beautiful bitch, La Roche, and invested heavily by purchasing Fashion, Ch. Thackeray Soda, Ch. Glen Monarch, Ch. General Donax, Rodney Clematis, Rodney Monarch, and many other winners.

Richard Croker of New York imported Ch. Rodney Stone from Mr Jeffries; it is stated by Watson that he paid $5,000 for the dog. He also imported Ch. Bromley Crib for which he is reputed to have paid $4,000, plus Ch. Petramose, Ch. Persimmon, Bit

of Bluff, Little Witch and others. At the Philadelphia show in 1901, the winning dog was Rodney Stone, followed by Katerfelto, Portland and Mersham Jock. Vandergrift withdrew from showing thereafter.

As the breed grew in popularity many exhibitors continued to import Champion dogs from the well-known English kennels and some of the best dogs of the time found their way over the Atlantic, which laid the sound foundation of the breed and its tremendous success enjoyed in the USA at the time.

1940s: Am. Ch. Cockney Gorblimey.

1950s: Eng. Am. Ch. Juneters Ace.

BULLDOG CLUBS

The Bulldog Club of America's constitution and bye-laws were amended in 1904 and the club was incorporated and then recognised by the American Kennel Club as the parent club for all Bulldog specialty clubs. It held two shows a year, one in New York and another in Philadelphia. It steadfastly opposed giving its approval for the creation of other Bulldog clubs until 1907 when it recognised the Bulldog Club of Philadelphia. The Board of Governors decided that the BCA should act as a national club and would hold its specialty shows in different parts of the country from year to year. The club has maintained this policy to the present day.

TOP DOGS

Americans continued to import Bulldogs from Britain but on 29 September 1967 at the BCA Specialty Show held in Plainview, New York, the Best of Breed winner was Dr Edward M. Vardon's Ch.Vardona Frosty's Masterpiece. Shortly after this win, he was exported to England, thus reversing the trend.

It would be amiss not to mention some of the top-winning Bulldogs in the USA over the years. Many a good one will be missed out, as there are too many to mention in the scope of this book, so here are a few dogs that, in the writer's opinion, would have won anywhere in the world.

LEADING AMERICAN BULLDOGS

The date given by each dog is when they achieved Championship status.

1930s
- Ch. Basford Ideal, 1936

1940s
- Ch. Cockney Gorblimey, 1945
- Eng. & Am. Ch. Marquis of the Hills, 1949

1950s
- Ch. Helmer's Beau Gay, 1950
- Eng. & Am. Ch. Juneters Ace, 1950
- Ch. Wiskehob Lord Calvert, 1952
- Ch. Sir Reilly of Kilarney, 1953, top-winning US-bred Bulldog
- Int. Ch. Banshee of Beechlyn, 1954
- Eng. Am. Ch. Kippax Dreadnought, 1954, Top Dog, Top Sire
- Eng. Am. Ch. Kippax Fearnought, 1954, BIS Westminster
- Ch. Vardona Frosty Snowman, 1959

1960s
- Ch. Sandows Smasher, 1963

1970s: Eng. Am. Ch. Dey Del.

1980s: Am. Ch. Cherokee Yancey.

- Ch. Estrid Jupiter, 1965
- Ch. Heatherbull Arrogance, 1965
- Ch. Dickensbrae Silver Spurs 1967

1970s
- Ch. Sourmug's Jon Jon, 1971
- Ch. Eng. & Am. Ch. Dey Del,
- Ch. Jonathon of Riverbrae, 1972
- Ch. JC's Jon Boy Collins, 1974
- Ch. Taurus Trailblazer, 1974
- Ch. Dingman's Hunk of Heatherbull, 1977
- Ch. Marinebull All the Way, 1978

1980s
- Ch. Beauty's Essex, 1980
- Ch. Bowag' s Arthur De Day, 1983
- Ch. Melrod's Fabulous Freddy, 1984
- Ch. Smasher's Al Capp, 1984
- Ch. Cherokee Yancey, 1985
- Ch. Bowag's Po'lar, 1986

- Ch. Hug-O-Bull Ridgefield Calypso, 1986
- Eng. & Am. Ch. Jackath Silver Cloud, 1986
- Ch. Hug-O-Bull's Redskin Rhumba, 1988
- Ch. Kozabull Glynbourne Zeke, 1988
- Ch. Heatherbull Bounty's Frigate, 1989, over 52 BIS wins
- Ch. Cherokee Daniel Boone, 1989
- Ch. Tiffany's Mary Beth, 1989

1990s
- Ch. Cherokee Otis, 1990
- Ch. Dygros Gilbert, 1990
- Ch. Graybull's Alpine White Lace, 1990
- Ch. Tiffany' Tiger Lilly, 1990
- Ch. Millcoat's Titus, 1991
- Ch. Satuit Windjammer, 1991
- Ch. Tsar's Fat Man's Finale, 1991
- Ch. Resolute Daffodil, 1993
- Ch. Juggernaut Jubilee, 1993

- Ch. Newcombe's Desert Victory, 1993, No.1 Bulldog
- Ch. Elroston Snow White, 1995

THE NEW MILLENNIUM
- Ch. Beauties Amos, 2000
- Ch. Fantasies Galadriel, 2002, BOB BCA Specialty
- Ch. Resolute Sunrise Polaris, 2000
- Ch. Resolute Magic Dragon, 2000
- Ch. Adamant Warlock, 2005, No.1 Bulldog 2005
- Ch. Mytoys Mighty Colors of the Wind, 2006, BOB BCA Specialty
- Ch. Hug-O-Bull Lady Priscilla, 2007
- Ch. Legacy Take Me To The Copa, 2007
- Ch. Silverspoon's Nothing Personal, 2007, No.1 Bulldog
- Ch. Silverpoon's Just Peachy, 2008
- Ch. Mytoys Mighty Winds of Change, 2009

1990s: Am. Ch. Tsar's Fat Man Finale.

1990s: Am. Ch. Newcombe's Desert Victory.

Am. Ch. Adamant Warlock: Number One Bulldog 2005.

Am. Ch. Silverspoon's Just Peachy: A top winning American Bulldog 2008.

LEADING KENNELS

In the last 10 years or so, some of the most influential Bulldog kennels in the USA, which have been consistent in breeding type and influencing the breed generally, are: Adamant Bulldogs (Jennifer and Jay Joseph), Cherokee Bulldogs (Cody Sickle), Hug-O-Bull Bulldogs (Norma, Frank and Elizabeth Hugo), Imperious Bulldogs (Kelly and Rick Franz), Little Ponds Bulldogs (Elizabeth and Dan Karshner), Mouser's Bulldogs (Donna and Rick Mouser), Resolute Bulldogs (Dorothy and Julian Prager), Silverspoon's Bulldogs (Mary Aiken and Rick Sturiza), Tiffany Bulldogs (Lillian Tiffany), Warmvalley Kennels (Lynnsie Shea and Diane Wallwork).

There are, of course, many others that have been omitted due to lack of space and it is also pleasing to note that young, enthusiastic newcomers to the breed are determined to be added to this elite list. Bulldogs were ranked number 10 in 2007 (the first time in the top 10 in almost 75 years), and there were 22,160 Bulldog puppies registered out of 9,799 Bulldog litters registered and 23,413 in 2008, making them the eighth top breed. Popularity for the breed is at an all-time high.

WORLDWIDE STANDING

In the UK the breed is becoming very popular indeed, there were 3,975 Bulldog puppies registered in 2007 compared to 2,012 in 1998, and 4,217 Bulldog puppies in 2009.

Today, Bulldogs have become very popular all over Europe, in Central and South America, Japan and many other countries in Asia. Bulldog clubs are flourishing in many countries and the demand for puppies has never been higher. Fortunately, due to careful selection and breeders being more aware of genetics, Bulldogs today are healthier than their 19th-century ancestors. In fact, the 21st century Bulldog is even healthier than his 20th century predecessor. Provided breeders continue to put health above any other quality, there is little reason to worry about the future of this marvellous breed.

A BULLDOG FOR YOUR LIFESTYLE

Chapter 3

The Bulldog, like a number of the other bull breeds, such as the Boston Terrier, the Boxer, the Bullmastiff, and the French Bulldog, is known as a brachycephalic breed. A breed is defined as brachycephalic when the head of the dog is nearly as broad from side to side as from front to back, especially where the cephalic index – the ratio of the breadth of the head to its length, expressed as a percentage – is over 80 per cent.

The brachycephalic breeds have a number of unique characteristics when compared to the multitude of pedigree dogs available, which number over 200 in the UK, and over 400 in the USA. However, with these unique characteristics come a number of very particular demands. If you are considering acquiring such a breed, and in particular a Bulldog, you must give careful consideration beforehand as to whether or not it is going to be the right breed for you and your lifestyle.

A PERSONAL VIEW

As someone who has been breeding and showing brachycephalic dogs for nearly 40 years – initially Boxers and more recently Bulldogs – I wondered how I could find a way of helping people to choose a Bulldog to suit their lifestyle. I also felt slightly daunted by the fact that, in this modern age, there are so many different lifestyles. However, a discussion with the editor of this book confirmed that he wanted all of the contributions to the book to be "written from the heart" so that it would be different to most of the other 'standard' books and make its own unique contribution. This appealed to me, and so the challenge was accepted. However, in doing so it should be recognised that by writing the chapter from the heart, I am presenting a very personal opinion that comes from living with Boxers and Bulldogs for 40 years. As such, I have no doubt there will be many who disagree with some of what I say, but so be it and here goes!

BULLDOGS AS INDIVIDUALS

By necessity the content of this chapter needs to be written in general terms, reflecting what is considered to be the 'normal' nature and characteristics of a Bulldog and what lifestyle suits him best. However, it is critical that the reader understands that not all Bulldogs are alike and, as is true in all purebred breeds, a good number of puppies do not grow up to fit what is considered the 'norm' for their breed. So be aware that if you acquire a

Bulldog puppy, you cannot have absolute certainty as to what he will grow up to be like. You can have reserved Bulldogs and Bulldogs who adore anyone; lively Bulldogs and calm, placid Bulldogs; no-messing Bulldogs and sweet-natured Bulldogs; serious Bulldogs and good-natured 'idiots'! Nevertheless, remember that your lifestyle and how you raise and treat your Bulldog will undoubtedly have a major impact on how he eventually turns out.

Taking on a dog of any breed is a major undertaking.

TAKING THE PLUNGE

So if you think you want to acquire a dog, and possibly a Bulldog, what is the first step you should take? Consider the following:

- Whether you want a male or female, puppy or adult
- The size of dog best suited for your environment
- What coat length and type you would prefer
- What temperament would suit you best
- Whether you want a pedigree or crossbreed
- Whether you want one or more dogs (the general advice is that two together is a bad idea)
- The impact of any existing dogs you may have.

GENERAL BULLDOG CHARACTERISTICS

If you are convinced you want a medium-sized companion dog that:

- Will constantly want to keep you and your immediate family company
- Is at his happiest when he is living indoors, preferably lying flat on the floor on a cushion or on a bed, staring happily at members of the family
- Has a fantastically sweet nature and wants to share every part of daily activities with his family members
- Despite his loving, friendly nature shows great courage in protecting his adopted family

and has physical characteristics whose deterrent effect should not be underestimated
- Does not need an excessive amount of exercise and is usually happier with a limited amount of exercise but at regular intervals
- Is very intelligent with lots of common sense that results in him examining every command you give him before deciding whether it is a worthwhile thing to do, and consequently has a reputation for stubbornness
- Has a short, easy-to-maintain coat that comes in a wide variety of colours

then a Bulldog may well be the right choice for you, as all of the above are undoubtedly considered normal characteristics of the modern Bulldog.

SPECIFIC BULLDOG CHARACTERISTICS

You should now take a much closer look at the very specfic characteristics of a Bulldog and decide if you are the right owner for a Bulldog. You must be absolutely sure that you can provide a Bulldog with the right type of environment and lifestyle before you proceed to acquire one, and in order to do this, you need to consider a significant number of characteristics that are very specific to the Bulldog.

NATURE AND APPEARANCE

I would strongly recommend that one of the very first things you consider is whether or not the Bulldog's nature and looks will really suit you and your family. There can be no avoiding the fact that Bulldogs were first developed in the early 19th century with the sole purpose of fighting/attacking bulls, bears and other animals in the arena for so-called 'sport', often with the involvement of betting. As such they were bred for their ferocious, aggressive and blood-thirsty nature, with many physical characteristics that supported their specific role in life. The nature of the original Bulldog was such that the Romans had a decree that forbid people taking one through the streets – even on a lead!

Regrettably, this frequently leads to the press and other media of today continuing to portray the Bulldog as an aggressive dog, as well as often linking, or confusing, the modern Bulldog with other breeds that continue to exhibit fighting and/or aggressive characteristics. This is disappointing when the reality is that, following the outlawing of bull-baiting in Great Britain in 1835 and many years of dedication and commitment by Bulldog breeders, nothing could be further from the truth.

Today's Bulldog, while maintaining many of the physical characteristics of the original Bulldog that give him a unique and immediately recognisable appearance, now has an unbelievable personality that makes him a great canine companion. However, most people either love or hate Bulldogs, which is probably true for most, if not all of the brachycephalic breeds. This arises because of the construction of the head, and the resulting position of the eyes, which means that this type of dog looks at you straight on (as humans do)

and you are either comfortable with this or not. You should therefore give this particular point careful consideration and discuss it with the rest of the household before you make a final decision.

If you all agree that you really do want a Bulldog, it is also important to recognise that in light of the media's tendency to completely misrepresent today's Bulldog, it is the prime responsibility of all Bulldog owners to represent and promote the many virtues of the Bulldog's impeccable nature.

The Bulldog is a breed that arouses strong passions.

The peace of your home may be shattered by a Bulldog's snores...

FLATULENCE

Without any doubt, most Bulldogs have a propensity towards an active gastrointestinal system and this results in the frequent, regular passing of wind. This is normal for them and is of no harm to them, but you need to consider whether or not it will offend you, as well as any guests you may have. So, if you have a pristine, sweet-smelling home and want to keep it that way, then a Bulldog is probably not for you!

There are a number of proprietary foods now available on the market that claim to help reduce this particular Bulldog trait, although I must say that, having tried one or two of them, they don't make that much difference. However, it is also my experience that where the situation allows Bulldogs to be fed a natural diet of meat and other fresh foods, it does alleviate the problem to some extent.

SNORING

Another unique characteristic of the Bulldog is that he tends to sleep more contentedly than many other breeds and this, when combined with the construction of his head, probably explains their penchant to snore rather loudly. The sound of a snoring Bulldog is endearing to some people but nerve-wracking to others. You therefore need to consider whether or not the snoring is going to bother you, or anyone else in the family; if it is, then I strongly recommend that you choose another breed. Personally, I find nothing more relaxing than listening to the sound of a houseful of Bulldogs snoring away, invariably in consort!

SLOBBERING

The Bulldog has a tendency to slobber and drool, especially after eating or drinking, and if he shakes his head, the saliva will travel an unbelievable distance and require the cleaning of your clothes, furniture, floors and walls! Although the amount of slobber is not so prevalent these days, following the refinement that has taken place to the head of the modern Bulldog, it does still occur on a fairly regular basis so, once again, if you have a pristine home and want to keep it that way, then a Bulldog is probably not for you!

LIFE EXPECTANCY

The average life expectancy of a Bulldog is around 8-10 years, although some will undoubtedly live much longer. Our oldest is currently almost 12 and still going strong, even after a major operation at 10 years of age to remove a large ovarian tumour. However, if you really must have a long-lived dog then a Bulldog is probably not for you.

CHEWING

When not playing, being exercised or resting, Bulldogs love something to chew – and because of the strength in their jaws, they can chew through almost anything! They have a definite panache for finding amusement in tearing up discarded waste left within their reach, chewing on slippers, shoes and furniture, and a number of other mischievous indoor adventures. The easiest way to avoid this problem is to not put temptation in their path, to train them from a puppy to understand that they have their own specific playthings, and to provide them with a lot of chew toys. I find that nylon bones (Nylabones) are best for Bulldogs because they take at least a little time to be destroyed and do not get caught in their throat as many other dog toys can. Whatever you do, do not give them small bones that can easily splinter. If you do not want to take the risk of having furniture damaged in the rooms where your dog will have access, a Bulldog is not for you.

MAKING THE COMMITMENT

So if after considering the breed's unique characteristics and deciding you are the right owner for a Bulldog, what are going to be the main issues that will impact on your lifestyle?

KNOWLEDGE/KNOW HOW

The Bulldog is not by nature a demanding breed, but he really does need his adopted family to have a sound knowledge of the breed, and, in particular, his health-care requirements. This can be gained by reading a number of books on the breed and talking to others more experienced in owning the breed. Once you have your own Bulldog, you will, of course, acquire your own hands-on practical experience – and you will never stop learning about Bulldogs when you spend your life with them.

HOME SET-UP

The Bulldog is one of the most accommodating breeds and will adapt to varying home set-ups and lifestyles, be it rural, city, mansion, cottage, terraced and even a flat. There is, however, one cautionary note if you live in a flat and are going to buy a

COST OF OWNERSHIP

You will need to understand and appreciate that the Bulldog is not a 'cheap' breed, so unless you are absolutely sure that you can afford the initial and subsequent ongoing outlay, do not proceed to acquire one. The main costs you will need to consider are:

- Purchase price: At the time of writing, the purchase price of puppies is between £1,500-£2,000.
- Daily feeding: The Bulldog is not a giant breed so does not consume huge quantities of food, but he must be fed a good-quality, well-balanced diet.
- Accessories/equipment: There will be the initial investment to provide suitable accommodation. The amount you spend on other equipment is largely a matter of

personal choice.
- Training classes: The weekly fees to attend a training class are modest, but it is important to take it on board so your Bulldog is properly socialised.
- Boarding kennels: You may need to use the services of boarding kennels for holidays or to cover unforeseen situations, such as hospital stays.
- Vet fees: The Bulldog is a man-made breed and his particular conformation means that you need to pay more attention to his health care, which may involve more frequent trips to the vet than with some of the tougher, working breeds.
- Dog insurance: The potentially high veterinary costs associated with Bulldogs means that taking out insurance may be a sensible option.

Bulldog. If your flat is not on the ground floor, consider seriously how you will get 55 lbs plus (24 kgs) of dog in and out of the apartment if the lift fails. Bulldogs are not designed to walk up or down multiple flights of stairs, and they do need to go outside!

WORK SCHEDULE
Despite his accommodating nature, the one thing a Bulldog *must have* is companionship, and this requirement starts from the first day that he enters over your threshold, particularly if he is a

puppy. A Bulldog hates spending hours alone, especially when young, and if he is left alone, chewing from boredom is the likely outcome. Many Bulldogs end up in rescue because new owners fail to understand and address this fundamental requirement.

I, personally, will not sell a Bulldog puppy (or even an adult) to anyone who lives on their own, is working full-time and cannot make suitable, reliable arrangements to ensure their Bulldog is not left for more than a

maximum of three to four hours.

If you work full-time and money is not a key issue, it is now possible, for a cost, to arrange for a pet sitter and/or dog walker. Over the past few years a wide selection of providers of this type of service has entered into the market, and an internet search will soon identify the providers in your local area. However, if you should decide to adopt this option, you must ensure that the provider is appropriately qualified and has the relevant experience.

It is a bonus if you can take your Bulldog on holiday.

HOLIDAYS

It is a fact that the overriding majority of Bulldogs do not enjoy going into boarding kennels. If you are therefore keen on going away for short or long breaks in the UK, it is advisable to train your dog from a young age to sleep in a crate so that he can go with you. Many hotels, holiday cottages and camp-sites now welcome dogs trained to sleep in crates in your accommodation, and your Bulldog will be a lot, lot happier being with you rather than in a boarding kennel.

The other options you can consider are:

- **Private Boarding:** Your Bulldog will stay in a private home with an animal carer. Providers offer one-to-one care for your Bulldog, and he will live pretty much as a family pet.
- **Home boarding:** Your Bulldog will remain at home in his usual environment and an experienced animal carer will live in your home and sleep there overnight.

For shorter periods away from home there are a number of additional options:

- **Pet sitting at home:** Here a carer will sit with your Bulldog(s) at home for an agreed number of hours during the day and/or evening.
- **Puppy care at home:** With this option your Bulldog puppy is visited in his home and the carer remains for a designated period to play, feed and toilet train.
- **Dog walking:** A dog handler will walk your Bulldog(s), usually on a one-to-one or

two-to-one basis, for a specified period. This can be on a regular or ad hoc basis.

- **Doggie day care:** Your Bulldog will spend a day in a carer's home that operates like a children's crèche. This can be on a regular or ad hoc basis.

SECURITY

Despite his appearance, the Bulldog is not intended to be a guard dog. In fact, the majority of Bulldogs will leave with anyone who will take them! With the high purchase cost of a Bulldog, this has led to a worrying increase in their theft. It will therefore be necessary for you to ensure that you have a secure, fenced garden for when your dog is outdoors.

CARING FOR YOUR BULLDOG

Caring for a dog of any breed requires a considerable commitment in terms of time, but with a Bulldog you need to take on board his unique temperament. The Bulldog is one of the most stoic of breeds, which means that a dog will often suffer in silence. You will therefore need to keep a very close eye on your Bulldog and spend some considerable time, on a regular and frequent basis, to help maintain and ensure his well-being.

ROUTINE CARE

In terms of grooming, the Bulldog is low maintenance compared to many other breeds, but he still needs a weekly brush. Attention must also be paid to the skin wrinkles on the head, which must be cleaned daily to avoid bacterial or fungal infections.

A number of Bulldogs have kinked tails that are very tight to the back end of the dog, which will necessitate daily attention to keep the base of the tail clean and from becoming moist.

DAILY EXERCISE

In general, Bulldogs will adapt very quickly to the amount of exercise you wish to give them, but, as a generalisation, they should be exercised daily and you will find that they are happier with regular walks of short to medium distance. Most sources recommend relatively short walks at a steady but not terribly brisk pace, totalling 20 to 40 minutes per day.

For more information on caring for your Bulldog, see Chapter Five: The Best of Care.

ACQUIRING YOUR BULLDOG

Having decided that a Bulldog really is for you and can be accommodated in your lifestyle with the necessary love and care, how do you go about acquiring one?

The first thing you need to decide is what do you want from your Bulldog? Purely a companion or one that can be shown as well? A puppy or an adult? A male or a female?

The Bulldog does not need as much exercise as some of the working breeds, but he should be kept fit with regular outings.

COMPANION OR SHOW?

The vast majority of Bulldogs are sold as companion animals where they will often be the only dog in the family. It is also a fact that many owners, having acquired a Bulldog as a companion, then get introduced to the fascinating and rather contagious world of dog showing and go on to acquire one or more Bulldogs for show as well as companionship.

Many Bulldogs sold purely as companion animals are more than capable of holding their own in the show ring and it is said that there are more 'potential' Champion Bulldogs sat at home in front the fire than there are actually in the show ring. I believe this to be true.

However, if you want a guaranteed show dog, the only way you can be absolutely sure of achieving this is by buying an older animal and not a young puppy. This is because Bulldogs are very slow to mature. While the majority of pedigree breeds mature between 12 to 24 months, the Bulldog is closer to 36 months before he 'finishes'. In the light of the many 'beauty' points that go to make a successful show dog – all of which can change and 'go wrong' during the development phase – no breeder can guarantee you a show puppy. Therefore, the phrase usually used by breeders if you ask them for a show puppy is that the puppy they are selling you has 'show potential'.

There is no guarantee that a puppy with show potential will mature into a successful show dog.

PUPPY OR ADULT?

As stated in the previous paragraph, if you want a Bulldog that is suitable for showing (and possibly breeding), the purchase of a young adult from a reputable and experienced breeder will provide you with greater certainty with respect to quality. However, even if you just want a companion Bulldog, you should still consider whether or not an adult dog would be better for you than a puppy. The advantages of acquiring an older dog are:

- What you see is what you get!
- It eliminates the many problems involved in raising a puppy.
- An older dog is usually already house-trained.
- An adult will 'relocate' to a new home extremely well as

long he is given all the love and attention he needs.
- He will require significantly less supervision and control of such activities as chewing.

There are, however, potential disadvantages of purchasing an adult Bulldog rather than a puppy, which you should consider:

- An adult dog will invariably have developed social activities that may or may not fit into your lifestyle.
- An adult may not have lived with other animals and may find it impossible to adjust to an environment that includes other animals, particularly cats.
- An adult dog may never have lived with children and may not be able, or may take some

A male (right) is bigger, and sometimes more headstrong. A female tends to more protective of family and home.

time, to adjust to the unique environment that children create around them.

If you do decide to take on an adult dog rather than a puppy, I strongly recommend that you arrange to take on the dog initially on a trial basis to ensure the dog can adapt to your home and lifestyle.

MALE OR FEMALE?

As in all breeds, there are gender-related differences in Bulldogs and you should consider these before deciding whether or not you wish to acquire a male or female. However, as a generalisation, I believe that the pros and cons of each sex tend to balance each other out and the final decision to acquire a male or female Bulldog, be it puppy or adult, is an individual choice and very much down to personal preference.

The key issues to consider with a male Bulldog are:

• They are usually bigger in size, weight, and their physical 'presence'.

• They provide a better deterrent to any potential threat to family and household due to their larger size.
• They cock their legs when urinating and any upright object that has any resemblance to a post or wall is considered fair game.
• They tend to be more headstrong and therefore can take longer to learn the rules.
• They may be more aggressive, especially around other males. This is particularly true if they have been used at stud.

The key issues to consider with a female Bulldog are:

• Unless you have the bitch spayed, she will come into season approximately every six months, although the timing between seasons can vary significantly with some bitches. Normally the season will last approximately three weeks, during which time she will have a bloody discharge from her vagina. The discharge is normally bloodier and heavier during the first 10 days, and the bitch may need to be confined if you are to avoid contaminating household furnishings. She also needs to be kept well away from any male dogs throughout the period of the season if you are to avoid an unwanted pregnancy.
• In my experience, if you have more than one Bulldog bitch and they 'fall out', you will have a problem for as long as

It may take some time to hunt down a litter produced by a reputable breeder.

you have the two bitches, even if they are mother and daughter!

- Bitches tend to be more family-oriented and protective of home and property, even though they are unable to match males for their physical presence.

FINDING A PUPPY

If you have decided that a puppy is what you want, then, as far as I am concerned, there is only one source that you should consider: a responsible breeder who consistently produces Bulldogs that are sound in construction, of excellent temperament, and come

from a healthy, stable environment. There is no doubt that if you want a healthy Bulldog puppy, then it is the breeder that is the most important consideration. If you take the time and trouble to find a responsible breeder, you stand the best chance of getting a Bulldog that will enjoy a happy and healthy life, and, in the long run, this will save you a lot of grief, time and money.

Whatever you do, unless you are accompanied by someone well experienced with Bulldogs, do not buy a puppy on impulse and/or from the first advert you see, even if it means that you

may then have to wait some time before you acquire your puppy. Also remember that reputation is far more important than ease of location and always read high-profile adverts with the knowledge that "good wine needs no bush". Not all reputable breeders run large kennels and the majority are, in fact, small hobby breeders who keep only a few dogs and have litters fairly infrequently. These hobby breeders are just as dedicated as the larger kennels to breeding quality Bulldogs, and they have the distinct advantage that they are able to raise their puppies in a home environment

The puppies should look like adults in miniature.

with all the accompanying attention and socialisation.

A reputable, established breeder will sell you a puppy at a sensible price, can be depended on to provide sensible advice at any time, and will take a puppy back within a reasonable time frame should you decide that it is not the right dog for you. However, you should also be aware that a reputable breeder will not sell you a puppy without first literally interrogating you and your family to determine your suitability to own and look after one of their puppies. Do not let this put you off, and, whatever you do, do not take the easier option to buy your puppy from a pet shop, puppy dealer or similar.

So what is the best way of going about finding a reputable breeder? I would recommend a combination of at least two of the following options:

- **Word of mouth/personal recommendation.** If you know someone who already has a Bulldog and it is a fit and healthy companion, with an excellent temperament, then discuss with them where they bought it, how helpful the breeder was, any problems they have experienced etc. If they recommend the breeder, then make contact and see if you can arrange a visit to their kennel.
- **Kennel club and breed clubs.** The majority of kennel clubs responsible for overseeing and governing dog activities in the different countries of the world maintain lists of local breed clubs and breeders. In most cases you can get these details readily via the internet.
- **Bulldog Breed Council.** In the UK, at the time of writing, there are 15 Bulldog clubs

spread across the country and 14 of these clubs are members of the UK Bulldog Breed Council. The Bulldog Breed Council has an excellent website, containing lots of useful information, including a list of the participating clubs and the names and contact details of the club secretaries. You are strongly recommended to visit the site before deciding on the purchase of your puppy.
Internet. A simple search on Bulldogs will also give you a large number of websites for individual breeders, often giving information about their stock, show wins, dogs for sale etc. From this source you should be able to find several breeders within a reasonable distance of your home.
- **Adverts/dog press.** Adverts in your local and national press, as well as in the papers published specifically for people with an interest with dogs, provide another potential source of details of Bulldog breeders.

Having made contact with several breeders, you will be in a position to decide the breeder that you believe will be the right one to provide the Bulldog puppy you desire. Be aware that many reputable breeders have waiting lists and it may be that you will have to wait for some time to buy a puppy from the breeder you have chosen. Most breeders usually allow potential buyers to visit the puppies when they are five to six weeks of age with a view to going to their new home from eight to 12 weeks, much depending on how quickly and how well they adapted to being weaned away from their mother.

If at all possible, take someone with you who is experienced in Bulldogs when you visit the breeder and their puppies so that you have some professional advice to ensure you do not just accept the first 'cuddly' puppy that you see but which could turn out to be a disaster.

ASSESSING THE PUPPIES

So what should you be looking for when you visit the breeder to consider picking your puppy? The puppy should be:

TYPICAL OF THE BREED

The puppy should be as close to the Breed Standard as possible, reflected by the fact that he should look like an immature adult Bulldog but with all of the key characteristics of the breed. Many experienced breeders believe, including me, that at eight weeks a puppy is a miniature of how the puppy will eventually end up as an adult. However, be aware that from eight weeks to maturity Bulldogs go through spurts of growth where various parts of the body appear to grow totally independent of each other. This can happen to such an extent, and so quickly, that the Bulldog puppy can look one way one day and completely different a week later.

Also remember that the perfect Bulldog has never been born and even the very best 'show potential' puppies will have some fault or other when compared to the Breed Standard. It is all a matter of degree. It is also true that while some faults would effectively stop your dog winning in the show ring, it would not stop him looking and behaving 100 per cent Bulldog and being your best companion ever. The breeder can only sell you a puppy with 'show potential'. If the breeder says anything else, be wary, especially if the price being asked for the puppy is higher than the norm.

If you are going to try to purchase a 'show potential' puppy without the help of someone who is experienced in Bulldogs, then, as a minimum, you will need to understand and be able to interpret the complex Bulldog Breed Standard, with its many nuances and how these should reflect in a young puppy. Space does not permit a long, detailed explanation here of what to look for in trying to select a show prospect puppy. However, a number of the key points to look for are:

The head: This is paramount – without correct head type, you do not have a Bulldog! The head should appear brick-shaped in outline when viewed from both the front and side. The top of the skull should be flat and broad with fine, not heavy, wrinkles.

The ears should be small and thin in order to achieve the

The head is a key feature of the breed.

required 'rose ear' shape (ears held back, showing the burr) by the time that the puppy gets to three to four months. However, if you are viewing puppies at six to eight weeks, it is likely that the ears will still be hanging forward in the 'button eared' shape. As long as the ears are small and thin, you should find that as the muscles in the ear strengthen, the ears will turn back of their own accord. The ears should be set high and placed as far apart as possible and as far from the eyes as possible.

There should be a clearly defined stop, from which a furrow should run to the apex of the skull.

The nose and nostrils should be large, broad and black.

The eyes and stop should be in the same straight line and wide apart, although the outer corners should be within the outline of the cheeks. Avoid any puppy that does not have round and very dark, almost black, eyes that show no white when looking directly forward.

The jaws should be broad and square, with the six small front teeth between the canines in an even row. When you look at the puppy's mouth straight on, the front under jaw should be

The breeder will 'stand' the puppy and will help you to assess his conformation.

directly under the upper jaw and parallel (i.e, not wry). You should not see any teeth when the mouth is closed.

The body: Look for a stocky puppy that is well boned, short in back with a roach that is not exaggerated, has a defined neck and has good front and rear angulation. Look for a good spring of rib. Avoid any puppy with a tail that is carried proud of the topline due to it being set too high and/or being held high (i.e. a gay tail).

Clean and healthy: This is probably the most important consideration of all. Check that the skin is supple and the coat soft, not harsh, and with no signs of fleas or other parasites. The ears should be pink and clean with no sign of a discharge. The

nose should be black, cold and wet with no discharge of any kind. The eyes should be dark and clear, again with no discharge. Teeth must be well formed, bright, clean and of good size. The wrinkles around the head and tail (top and bottom) should be clean and dry with no staining, sores or excess moisture.

Whatever you do, never, never choose a puppy that looks sickly, lethargic, nervous, overly frightened or has a cough and/or diarrhoea.

If you are accompanied by someone experienced in Bulldogs they will be able to advise you about poor conformation in a puppy as this can be relatively easily determined at eight weeks by an expert eye. If there is a 'runt of the litter', do not feel sorry for it and buy it.

Sound temperament: The puppies should be outgoing, mischievous and bouncy, with a happy and friendly manner. However, puppies in a litter can vary in temperament from totally passive to extremely dynamic, and you really need to pick the one with the temperament most suitable for your lifestyle. The really outgoing puppy may well

It is important to see the mother with her puppies, as this will give you some idea of how they might turn out.

turn out to be very headstrong and require that you have extreme patience and plenty of time to train him. It could well be that the more quiet and reserved puppy will be more suitable for you. There is nothing wrong with the quieter and reserved puppies so long as they do not show any signs of nervousness or fear.

MEETING THE FAMILY

Make sure you see the mother with her puppies. As described above, she should be typical of the breed, healthy, structurally sound, and of good temperament. Remember, though, that bitches invariably lose their coat after raising a litter of pups so she may well not be in

100 per cent condition. However, if the mother shows any signs of nervousness, aggressiveness or one or more significant structural faults, you would probably be better off not risking buying a puppy from this litter.

Also ask if the father of the puppies is available to be seen. If not, ask to see a picture of him. The same points that you need to consider with regard to the mother also apply to the sire. I suggest you also ask the breeder why they used the sire in question. The response to this will give you some indication as to whether or not the litter was part of a breeding programme aimed at improving the breed, or just the use of the 'dog around the corner' in order to try to

make a quick profit.

As a very rough generalisation, consider that the mother contributes 40 per cent to her offspring and the same applies for the father. You therefore tend to get quality puppies where both the mother and father are quality stock, although nature being what it is, there will, of course, always be exceptions to this, both ways.

In the UK, check that both the mother and father have been assessed through the Bulldog Breed Council health assessment scheme and ask if you can see the completed Health Certificate form, certainly for the mother, and, if at all possible, for the sire as well. Under the scheme the health assessment is carried out by a vet, 14 physical characteristics are assessed, and there is no overall pass or fail. However, a reputable breeder will take note of the assessment and use it to inform their future breeding programme. As a minimum, you would not expect to see a dog and a bitch mated if they both have the same fault noted on their assessment.

DETAILS OF THE LITTER

Determine if the puppies have been reared in a kennel or in the home. Smaller breeders invariably raise their puppies in the home environment, and this has the distinct advantage over kennel-reared puppies of providing considerably more personal attention and socialisation. A puppy that has been both well bred from sound stock and well socialised in the home environment will want nothing

more than to please and be near you and your family.

Find out how many puppies were in the litter and how many survived. If there was a high death rate, ask the breeder if there was a particular reason why this occurred. If it was disease related, check that all the surviving puppies have been cleared by a vet. The average litter size in Bulldogs is four to five puppies, although any number from one puppy to nine or 10 puppies frequently occurs.

Check how many puppies have already been booked. If you are purely looking for a pet puppy then the answer is probably of no real consequence, but if it is a puppy with 'show potential' that you are looking for, you really need to consider all the puppies in the litter and have the first pick, or, as a minimum, second pick.

ACQUIRING AN ADULT

If you have decided that you would prefer an adult Bulldog rather than a puppy, what are the sources available?

If your decision to purchase a more mature dog is to ensure, as far as is ever possible, that you have a Bulldog of show quality, then the only sensible way forward is to put yourself in the hands of one or more reputable breeders, ensuring that you explain fully your requirements to them. Be aware that it is likely you may well have to wait some time until a suitable dog becomes available and that even with an older Bulldog no one can give you an absolute guarantee regarding the dog's future show career.

If you want an adult Bulldog purely as a pet, then there are a number of potential sources you can consider. The main ones are:

A REPUTABLE BREEDER

Breeders are sometimes over-stocked and occasionally have an adult that they wish to place in a pet home because of one or more of the following reasons:

Sometimes a breeder may be over-stocked and will be willing to part with an adult.

- The dog has reached the end of its show career. These dogs are usually at least three or four years old.
- The dog is not required for the breeder's future breeding programme.
- The dog had been 'run on' by the breeder to assess his show potential, but, in the end, he did not made the grade. These dogs are generally around 12 months of age or less.

Most reputable breeders do not advertise any older stock that they may have available for a pet home and prefer to rely on word of mouth for finding a suitable home. It may therefore be worth contacting a number of breeders to determine if they have such an adult for placement. Many reputable breeders do not make a charge for any older animals that they place in a home, although you may be asked to make a contribution to a Bulldog rescue charity. You can also expect to be fully interrogated about the home you can provide as such dogs usually have a special place in the heart of the breeder, who is only letting the dog go because they believe it will be more comfortable living out the rest of its life in a family environment rather than in a kennel.

With good care and management, your Bulldog will soon become an integral member of the family.

RESCUED DOGS

Although it is difficult to imagine anyone abandoning or getting rid of a pet Bulldog, it is a fact of life that it sometimes happens and in most countries there is an active Bulldog rescue service in operation. Regretably, Bulldogs that end up in rescue may have behavioural or health problems and/or a history of ill treatment or neglect. You can therefore expect to be vetted and interrogated by the staff who run rescue service as to the suitability of yourself, your family, and your lifestyle for the Bulldog in question.

As far as the rescue service staff are concerned, the overriding priority is to establish that if a dog is placed in a home, he will not need to be moved on again, and that the environment is correct for the particular dog in question. You will also need to give very careful consideration to the dog's history and whether or not it is going to be suitable for you. Bulldogs that come through the rescue service frequently require a lot of extra work, and you should not consider a rescued dog if you have a very busy life and/or very young children. If a dog is placed with you, you can expect this to be on a trial basis and you must anticipate that there may be a settling-in period, both for you and the dog.

All-breed rescue services often have pedigree dogs available, but it is rare for them to have a Bulldog, as most go to the Bulldog rescue services, whichever country you live in.

IN SUMMARY

If, having considered carefully all of the guidance in this chapter, you have concluded a Bulldog is right for you, that he will fit into your lifestyle and that you can provide all the care and attention required, you will have no doubt proceeded to acquire one, hopefully also as advised in this chapter. Other chapters in this book will deal with how you should raise and look after your Bulldog once you get him home, and I have every confidence that if you also follow the advice in these chapters, you will have the most fantastic friend and devoted companion, and you will wonder how you ever managed to live without a Bulldog. Enjoy!

THE NEW ARRIVAL

Chapter 4

Before you bring your new Bulldog home, you need to be fully prepared for everything he is likely to need. This does not simply mean buying food, or a collar and lead, it is all about understanding your Bulldog's requirements. If you are bringing home a puppy, it is doubly important that you are prepared, and that your home and garden are completely puppy-proofed.

GARDEN SAFETY

A small puppy will find the smallest gap in the fencing, so walk all the way round the perimeter of your garden and check for any broken fencing or gaps where your puppy could squeeze through.

Ensure that any gates into the property can be locked from the inside and that the fencing itself is at least 6 ft (1.82 m) in height.

I know of many Bulldogs that can scrabble over a 3 ft fence (0.9 m), which many people do not expect. Panel fencing is good, but ensure you check it after any high winds, as it does tend to blow over easily. Chain-link fencing is fine unless there is a dog the other side of it that could arouse curiosity. Ensure there is at least a running board along the bottom to prevent either dog from scrabbling underneath it.

Garden ponds are always a danger – even the shallowest of ponds could be deep enough for a dog to drown in. If you cannot fence off the pond area, then fill it in. This may seem drastic, but, sadly, Bulldogs have been known to drown in ponds; the same applies to swimming pools. If you are using a cover, make sure it is a hard cover; the pull-over covers can create a hazard because if a dog falls in and goes under the cover, he will not be able to get

out again. Ensure that all sheds are secure and locked so that your Bulldog cannot gain access to insecticides, weed killers, anti-freeze, rodent killer, or other substances that are poisonous. There are also a number of garden plants that are poisonous to dogs. The most common include foxgloves and laburnum, as well as many of the spring bulbs.

IN THE HOME

Inside the house, ensure that all electric cables are tucked away and that anything you do not want chewed up is out of his reach. Breakable items should be removed, and, for the short-term, replace any expensive rugs with cheaper ones in case of accidents during the house-training period.

The home environment can be funfair of exciting things to play with, many of which are dangerous to your dog. As well as making sure that cables are not where they can be chewed, household cleaning products should also be kept in an area that your dog cannot access. It certainly helps to have an area in your home that is penned off, especially if you are bringing home a puppy. This can take the form of a stairgate across the kitchen door, restricting your puppy to one room, or you can use a puppy pen, which gives him his own special area safely away from any hazards when you cannot supervise him.

You also need to decide where your Bulldog is going to sleep. If you do not want him to sleep on your bed, than make sure he never has a chance to go there! Right from the start, decide where you want your puppy to be overnight. This may be in a crate, in a dog bed, in a puppy pen, in the kitchen or utility room, or the conservatory. Be aware that conservatories can become very hot during the summer months, and, conversely, they can be cold in the winter.

Once you have decided where your pup will be overnight, place him in his bed, go to bed yourself and ignore any cries. Be aware that this is the first night he will have been away from his

An inquistive Bulldog puppy will explore every nook and cranny of his new home.

littermates and it will be a bewildering time for him. Giving in and bringing him to bed will set a precedent for future nights and will prove a hard habit to break.

BUYING EQUIPMENT

CRATE
Investing in a crate is always worthwhile, as it not only gives you peace of mind, but it also provides a safe den for your puppy. It is important to buy a crate that will be large enough for an adult Bulldog. The recommended size is 30 ins x 20 ins x 24 ins (76 x 51 x 61 cm), which will fit on a show bench and in the back of most cars. Crates are not cruel, they provide a safe 'den' area for your dog (especially if covered), and

placing your dog in a crate at night is no more cruel than putting your baby in a cot.

The crate can be used both at night and during those times of the day when you cannot supervise your puppy. You can make it cosy by using synthetic fleece bedding. This is the best option, as, like a child's nappy, it soaks up moisture, keeping the top dry part for your puppy to sleep on. Cushion bedding is OK for adult dogs, but be aware that many Bulldogs wet their bedding and the larger cushion beds do not fit in the washing machine very easily. You can also buy a parrot bowl, which hooks on to the side of the crate. This allows you to provide fresh water and eliminates the risk of your puppy spilling his water all over his bedding.

PUPPY PEN
Many breeders use a puppy pen, and you may consider buying one of these so your pup has a play area where he will be safe when he is not being supervised. It serves the same purpose as a crate, but it gives the puppy more space so he can have a really good game with his toys. This provides a safe area for your dog to be if you are not home or overnight when you cannot supervise him.

BOWLS

You will need two bowls – one for food and one for water. It is best to buy those made of stainless steel rather than plastic, as they can be hygienically cleaned. I suggest you use eight-inch (20-cm) bowls for a puppy, and 10-inch (25.5-cm) bowls for an adult Bulldog. If you have laminate flooring, bowls with a rubber bottom are a good idea, as they do not slide across the floor so easily.

You can set up a carrier in a playpen so your puppy has a place to rest as well as having a play area.

FOOD

In the first few days after your puppy arrives in his new home, it is very important to feed the same food that was given to you by the breeder. You can gradually switch over to a different diet if you prefer at a later date, but, initially, stick with what your puppy is used to in order to avoid tummy upsets. Find out the breeder's timetable for meals, and try to stick to this regime, at least to begin with. It is also a good idea to buy mineral water, or boil water to begin with, as a change of water can upset a puppy's stomach. If you can remember to do so at the time you collect your puppy, ask the breeder for a bottle of local water so you can mix this in with your own water for the first few bowls of drinking water.

COLLAR AND LEAD/HARNESS

The type of collar and lead you buy is very much a matter of personal choice. For a puppy, a soft leather or nylon puppy set is idel in the early stages, when all you need to do is get him used to wearing a collar round his neck and become accustomed to the restrictions of walking on lead.

If you are taking on an older dog, try to find out what type of collar and lead, or harness, he has been used to. *Never* use a choke chain on a Bulldog: it constricts the neck, which is not only painful, but can damage the throat. If your adult Bulldog is prone to pulling on the lead, then a soft, nylon harness is much better, as it takes the pressure away from the throat, but also gives you a little more control over the dog. Occasionally you will find a Bulldog whose neck is as wide as his head; this type of dog will easily slip out of a collar, so a harness is the best option.

If you would rather use a collar, choose a soft, leather or nylon collar or preferably a half-check collar. These are half nylon and half chain, and they can be easily adjusted so they do not go any tighter than the size of your Bulldog's neck, but will allow you to tighten the collar fractionally if your dog is pulling without posing a choking hazard.

GROOMING KIT

The Bulldog is a low-maintenance breed in terms of grooming, but it is important that you keep the face folds and ears clean and dry.

You will need the following tools in your kit:

- A soft nylon brush or a rubber grooming mitt to keep the coat soft and clean. Brushing your Bulldog on a weekly basis is much better for the coat than bathing him too often. Over-bathing can strip the essential oils in the coat of the dog whereas brushing will stimulate these oils and keep the coat

PUPPY CARE

A puppy should get used to a care regime from the moment he arrives in his new home.

Wipe the ears clean, making sure you do not probe into the ear canal.

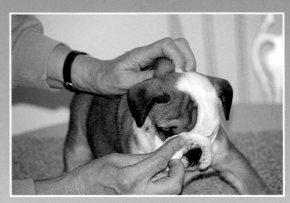

The nose roll must be dry and clean.

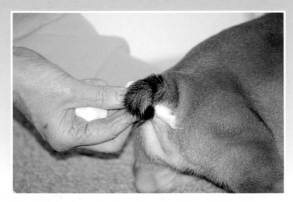

You will need to check under the tail, and wipe if necessary.

You may have to enlist extra help for nail-cutting.

naturally clean.

• A stripping blade or a furminator can be used to pull the dead fur from the base of the coat and will remove all the dead hair before brushing your dog with the nylon brush or rubber mitt. This is particularly useful if you have a white-coated Bulldog, which tends to moult a little more than, say, a red-coated dog.

• Nail-clippers. It is important to get your puppy used to not only having his nails cut but also having his feet handled. The standard dog nail-clippers are sufficient, but be careful not to cut through the quick of the nail. This can be more difficult on black nails, so a regular routine of just taking the tips off the nails is advisable. Sadly, once you cut through the quick of a nail, it not only bleeds profusely but can make cutting your dog's nails in the future a little more difficult, as he will tend to remember the experience.

Ensure you have a 'stop bleeding' product to hand just in case you do catch the quick.

- Unscented wet wipes for keeping the face folds clean, and also for cleaning under the tail. It is very important that you dry these areas thoroughly with cotton wool to prevent any infection or yeast build-up.

- Antiseptic cream for the face folds and for use under a tight tail; a shop-bought nappy-rash cream or a purpose-made canine antiseptic cream both work well and a daily routine of wiping the folds and smearing a little cream into them will prevent them from becoming sticky or infected.

- A purpose-made canine ear cleaner to keep the ears clean and free from wax and mites. Ears can quickly become waxy and ear infections can be difficult to get on top of, so ensure that you keep the ears clean on a regular basis to prevent any long-term ear problems.

- Vaseline, to keep the nose from drying out and becoming sore or for restoring a nose that is already dry and crusty. A regular smear on a weekly basis will help prevent a dry nose from forming and a smear several times a day over the course of a few days will quickly restore a dry nose. Be aware that the top layer of nose often comes away with the Vaseline if it has become very dry - this is normal and nothing to worry about.

TOYS

It is very important that you do not compromise by buying cheap toys. The Bulldog can be an aggressive chewer, so there is no point in buying soft, vinyl, squeaky toys, as they will be chewed to pieces in a matter of seconds – and, in some cases, the chewed-up toy could be swallowed and cause an intestinal obstruction.

Instead, ensure that the toys you buy are of a high grade and tough material designed specifically for dogs with a strong bite. Nylabones, Kong toys and similar are advised for the older Bulldogs, but for pups you can buy smaller toys – as long as they are robust.

Soft toys should only be considered if the eyes and nose parts cannot be removed by the dog; if they can, remove them yourself before giving them to your Bulldog. Young pups, especially those recently separated from their littermates, will appreciate having a soft toy to snuggle up to on those first few nights when they suddenly find themselves alone.

In all cases, keep a close watch on the toys and remove them as soon as they start to show signs of wear. Do *not* give your Bulldog rawhide in any shape or form. Sadly, many Bulldogs chew the rawhide to a soft slime and then attempt to swallow it, which

The toys you provide must be suitably robust.

could prove to be fatal if there is no one around to see it happen.

ID

In the UK, it is the law for all dogs to have some form of ID. Your dog must have a tag on his collar at all times in public places, including the car. It is not advisable to include the name of your dog on this tag, as it makes it too easy for a potential dog thief to call your dog away, but instead ensure it includes your name and your telephone number.

It is also strongly advised that your Bulldog is microchipped. If your breeder hasn't chipped your dog prior to being sold then make sure that you have it done as quickly as possible. The high

theft risk on this breed is a reason in itself why all dogs, especially those of high value, such as the Bulldog, should be microchipped. Also ensure that the information attached to the microchip is kept up to date – you can only be traced if your contact details are valid and bearing in mind that strays can legally be rehomed, or worse, destroyed after seven days, the need for a microchip in this day and age is absolutely paramount.

FINDING A VET

It's advisable that you have your new Bulldog seen by a vet within 48 hours of bringing him home. Many breeders' sales contracts insist this is done to ensure that the dog you have bought is

confirmed as being in good health at the time of purchase. Therefore it is wise to be registered with a vet before your Bulldog comes home.

Finding a vet is not as easy as it sounds. Sadly, many vets, especially the more newly qualified ones, are not Bulldog friendly and think nothing of telling the new Bulldog owner that they are going to have a lifetime of problems, even if the dog displays no obvious signs of ill health.

Ask friends you may know with a Bulldog if they can recommend a practice or contact your local breed club for advice. In the UK, both the Bulldog Breed Council and the Bulldog rescue websites have lists of Bulldog-friendly vets. If you know other Bulldog owners, ask them who they see; a vet who has experience of the breed is certainly a bonus. Once you have selected a possible practice, go and talk to the vet and form your own opinion. If you are happy with what you discover, book an appointment so your new dog can be checked over and microchipped, if necessary, once you have collected him.

COLLECTING YOUR BULLDOG

Arrange to collect your Bulldog as early in the day as possible to give him the maximum amount of time to settle into his new home before nightfall. This is a stressful time for your Bulldog puppy, especially if he is being separated from the rest of his litter.

It is important to find a vet who has experience of treating Bulldogs of all ages.

After all the hard work of rearing a litter, it is time for the puppies to go to their new homes.

When you go to the breeder, take a large towel so your pup can sit on your lap on the journey home. If you are collecting an adult dog, take a crate for him to travel in, or a harness that attaches to the seat belt. A loose dog in a car is not only dangerous if you have an accident, but you could also risk losing him if he tries to run away. If you are travelling home with a puppy, it is best to go straight home. Bearing in mind he will not be fully vaccinated, you will not be able to put him on the ground during any toilet breaks. If he has an accident, it will be absorbed in the towel. If you are collecting an adult, whether you need to stop is dependent on how far you have to travel.

Ask the breeder for a bottle of local water, which you can use as drinking water during the journey home, and to mix in with your own water once you get home, as a change in water can occasionally cause an upset tummy. You should also ask for a bag of whatever food your dog has been used to eating. A sudden change in diet can also cause tummy upsets, so even if you plan to feed something different, you will need a good amount of the existing food to mix in with it to prevent any sudden changes.

The breeder should also provide the following:

- A receipt.
- A five-generation pedigree. This is the 'family tree' for your puppy and sets out your puppy's ancestors over five generations, starting with the sire and dam (dad and mum).
- The registration documents proving registration of the puppy by the breeder with the governing kennel club for your country. This is your puppy's 'birth certificate'. When ownership of the puppy transfers from the breeder to you, the transaction is entered on the certificate, signed by both the breeder and yourself, and then sent to the appropriate kennel club, which will record on its computerised system that you are the new owner.
- A diet sheet informing you of the kind of food your puppy has been fed on, the amount and the frequency. The diet sheet should also advise you of the increases and changes in food that will be necessary week by week as your puppy matures.
- Details of when the puppy was last wormed and which product was used. You can then pass this information to

Try not to overwhelm your puppy when he first arrives home.

your vet, who will be able to advise you as to which wormer you should use and when.

• A contract of sale. This should set out clearly and succinctly the conditions under which the breeder is selling you the puppy, including both the breeder's and your responsibility to the puppy, and confirmation that the purchase of your puppy is contingent upon it passing an examination by your vet within a specified period (usually within 48 hours).
The contract should also list any official endorsements that the breeder placed on the puppy's records when it was registered with the appropriate kennel club, and on what basis

the breeder may be prepared to remove the endorsement(s). Although not frequently used, the endorsements more commonly placed on puppies by breeders include 'not for breeding' and 'not for export'. Before or at the time of sale, you will be required to give a signed acknowledgement of any endorsement placed. It should also state what should happen in the event you are unable to keep your puppy, either by returning it to the breeder or using the breed rescue.

• Written advice on training, exercise and immunisation, together with certificates for any vaccinations that the puppy has already had to date.

If any of the above documents are not available then be wary, very wary, before proceeding to buy a puppy.

ARRIVING HOME

Once home, it is important that you do not rush introductions with any existing dogs and members of your family, especially young children who can prove to be overwhelming in their excitement. I always say to let the dog find his feet at his own pace.

You may well have an area in the garden that you would prefer your puppy to toilet in, so it is wise to visit that spot as soon as you arrive home and praise him if he performs. If he does not, don't worry too much and certainly don't make it an issue, as toilet training needs to be kept as relaxed as possible in order for it to be efficient and successful.

If are bringing home a puppy, it is always worth having a separated area for him to call his own; this can either be a crate or a puppy pen, as mentioned earlier. The area should have bedding and water, and a variety of safe toys. Settle your puppy down, and then go and have a cup of tea. Allow an adult dog to explore at his leisure; once he feels safe and comfortable, he will come and find you.

Much of what we perceive as everyday stuff can be overwhelming to your little pup. The washing machine, cars out on the road, and screaming kids can suddenly feel like he has been dropped into a warzone –

especially for pups that were raised in a kennel environment. Take these early days slowly, and introduce him to his surroundings in a controlled manner.

MEETING THE FAMILY

It's not uncommon for members of your extended family to want to come and visit your new pup very quickly after he has arrived. Try to put them off for at least 24 hours to give him time to feel more secure in his new environment. Members of the existing family, especially children, will want to spend time with him, of course, but try to keep it to short bursts in an effort not to overtire your pup, as it's important that he gets sufficient sleep, especially as a young pup.

THE RESIDENT DOG

It is my experience that if you are bringing a second dog into your family, selecting one of the opposite sex is better than having two same-sex dogs. Two bitches tend to become bitchy around their seasons towards each other, and two males can become territorial, especially around the age of nine months when they receive a surge of testosterone that can turn them into lager louts.

Of course, it very much depends on the personality of the dogs involved, but it is wise to introduce two strange dogs on neutral ground. If you are introducing a pup, don't let him nag the resident dog as, if he sees the new arrival is a nuisance, it could instil early hostility.

SMALL ANIMALS

Cats, rabbits and other small animals can become a fascination for your puppy. It is quite normal for your dog to chase the cat, and equally as normal for your cat to hiss and strike out at the dog. In most cases the lesson will be learned. But you need to ensure that any interaction between your new Bulldog and any small animals is closely supervised.

THE FIRST NIGHT

The first night is often the hardest; you must allow your puppy to sleep where you will always require him to sleep – only allow him on your own bed if that is your plan for the rest of his life. Harden your heart and ignore his cries; going to a crying puppy will teach him that you are at his beck and call.

Ensure that the pup has emptied his bowels and his bladder before going to bed and settle him down in his pen or crate or wherever you have decided he is going to sleep at

A puppy will protest at being left on his own at night – but eventually he will learn to settle.

night. A soft toy (with eyes and nose removed) may well be appreciated to snuggle up to in the absence of his littermates. I do not advise providing him with a hot-water bottle in case the puppy chews it, allowing the hot water to scald him or make the bed area sodden. Make sure there is an area with newspaper for your dog to go to the toilet on during the night, and, once you have settled him, leave him until the morning so he learns that night times are for sleeping and not for playing.

HOUSE-TRAINING

Teaching your Bulldog to be clean in the house is much easier than you might think. It is all about routine – creating a routine and sticking to it! Give lots of praise when he goes outside and performs, and ignore accidents in the house, and he will soon understand what is required. It is especially important that you go outside with your dog so you can give the appropriate praise at the appropriate time. Simply opening the door and sending the dog out can prove to be non-productive, as he will probably sit by the door and wait to be let back inside.

Newspaper on the floor will help in the early days, especially overnight or when you need to leave your pup for any length of time – although this should never be longer than four hours. As he grows and becomes more used to holding his bladder, you can slowly decrease the area of newspaper.

Make sure you use the same 'emptying' command each and every time you need him to go to the toilet - "Be clean", "Do wee wees", "Hurry up" or whatever you are comfortable saying is fine as long as you keep to the same command. If you want the dog to use the same area in the garden then, initially, take him to that area, place him on the ground and use the chosen command. If he does not perform, make no issue of it whatsoever. If he does, give lots of praise so he knows he did the right thing.

Dogs learn by association, so many of these first experiences will be remembered. That is why accidents indoors are best ignored, because shouting may not only teach your puppy that spending in the house is wrong – it could also teach him that spending in front of you is wrong, and that will lead to great difficulties with house-training in the future. As a routine is established, things will become easier, but in those early day accept that your puppy cannot hold his bladder all night.

HANDLING

It is important that your puppy gets used to being handled all over. He should tolerate having his feet touched, his ears looked at, his teeth examined, and being groomed. With pups, ensure they become used to having their ears cleaned out from the very beginning. Infected ears are painful, so check them on a weekly basis and clean them out with a

Take your puppy out at regular intervals and he will soon learn what is required.

cotton-wool ball and a purpose-made canine ear cleaner.

If you can make sure this kind of all-over handling is accepted at an early age, it will be much easier to do as an adult. This is especially true if your Bulldog needs to be examined by a vet. In fact, it helps to go for an occasional visit without actually seeing the vet, so your puppy has a positive first experience and doesn't just associate the vet with being manhandled or being made to feel uncomfortable.

HOUSE RULES

It is important that you have house rules from day one. Bulldogs are clever – clever enough to pretend they are stupid, so anything that they get away with will be remembered and used again. Do not allow an eight-week-old pup to do anything that you would not allow a fully grown Bulldog to do. Remember that once fully grown, your Bulldog will weigh anything up to 30 kgs (66 lbs) – an average 25 kgs (55 lbs), so while a small pup can be picked up and carried away from an unsuitable situation, it will not be so easy once your dog is the size of a house with the brains to match.

If you do not want your Bulldog on the furniture, then prevent him doing so as a pup; the same applies to your bed and any room in the house that you wish to be dog-free. These early house rules are important, as it is easy to forget just how big he is going to get and it is very unfair and confusing for your dog to suddenly find that he can no longer do something he has been allowed to do in the past.

SUMMING UP

Above all, enjoy your Bulldog, and ensure he becomes an integral member of the family. This is a dog that is very good at knowing when you are happy and when you are sad; he knows how to make you laugh and how to make you angry. He is clever enough to have you waiting on his every whim – and, in no time at all, you will realise why we love the Bulldog as much as we do. With a face perfectly shaped for kissing and a body perfectly shaped to keeping your feet warm on a long winter's night, there is no doubt that once you have owned a Bulldog, you will never want any other breed.

Establish the house rules from day one, so your puppy learns acceptable behaviour.

THE BEST OF CARE

Chapter 5

To keep your Bulldog at his best, he needs a little more attention to detail than some other short-coated breeds, so it is important to ensure that he receives the best of care in all sectors of his life.

THE FOOD HE NEEDS

The basis of good care for a domestic dog is his food. The dog is an omnivore, so he can eat a variety of diets as long as they are balanced to meet his nutritional needs. Typically, a Bulldog diet requires: fats, carbohydrates, proteins, vitamins, minerals and water. He needs the right amount of calorific value for the amount of energy he expends, and his food needs to be palatable and nutritious.

Just like us humans, every Bulldog has individual feeding requirements, so a method that suits one Bulldog may not suit

another, even in the same household. As I write this, we have five Bulldogs eating four different types of food! So when you settle on a food regime for your Bulldog, you may still have to adjust it slightly to suit him completely.

UNDERSTANDING NUTRIENTS

A Bulldog needs a well-balanced diet that includes all the essential nutrients:

- **Fats:** These are the source of energy for a dog and, together with fatty acids, provide vitamins A, D, E, and K. They also maintain a healthy skin and coat.
- **Carbohydrates:** These are another source of energy and can be found in starches, sugars and dietary fibre, and can be sourced from plants or milk. Dietary fibre also affects the speed in which food intake passes through the system. Too

great an amount of milk-based carbohydrate can cause diarrhoea.

- **Proteins:** These are required for the regulation of metabolism, growth and maintenance of tissues, and they also provide essential amino acids. They are sourced from eggs, milk, meat, fish cheese and cereals. During growth stages and pregnancy, the protein levels for your Bulldog need to be higher than their normal intake.
- **Vitamins:** These are organic compounds that are essential to regulate metabolic processes and, while they are needed, as much harm can be done by over-dosing as not giving any.
- **Minerals:** There are 12 types that are essential for various body processes but, just like the vitamins, care must be taken not to over-dose your Bulldog on them.

A supply of fresh drinking water should always be available.

If you are feeding a complete diet, both vitamins and minerals will have been carefully added and no further supplementation is required. If you are feeding a homemade, natural or BARF (bones and raw food) diet, it would be wise to ask your veterinary surgeon for his advice on the matter.

WATER

Bulldogs require a plentiful supply of clean, fresh water at all times, and, as they are prone to leave saliva in their water bowls after a drink, be prepared to clean and change their water bowls several times a day.

DIETARY CHOICES

As a Bulldog owner, there are two routes to feeding that you can

choose from. There are the commercial foods, which come in different forms – the complete 'all in' kibble or muesli food, or canned, pouched, chubbed **(reformed)** food or semi-moist food. Or there is the home-prepared diet using either fresh meat or frozen fresh meat and there is also the BARF diet.

COMPLETE

There are many varieties and brands of complete dog food, even one specifically for Bulldogs, so it is a matter of what suits your dog and personal preference as to which you choose. Some owners prefer to serve the kibble soaked, as they feel it reduces the dangers of over-swelling in the stomach. If you opt to do this, you must use cold water, as hot will render any vitamins useless. If you soak a complete food, however, you lose the teeth-cleaning, crunchy properties of the kibble.

When choosing a complete food for your Bulldog, larger kibbles are best, as he can lose

The 'dry' or 'complete' diet caters for all your Bulldog's nutritional needs.

smaller ones from the side of his mouth as he eats. If fed on a complete diet, a Bulldog keeps his condition better on a lower protein brand – somewhere around 20 per cent is ideal. Quantities should be as the manufacturer's instructions.

The canned, pouched, chubbed and semi-moist foods are usually served with a suitable mixer and, again, the manufacturer's advice should be followed. All the commercial foods are easy to source and quick and simple to prepare.

HOME-MADE

To feed your Bulldog a home-made diet, you need to ensure you have the time and commitment to prepare his meals. You need to work out the correct portions for him to achieve all his nutrients, and to source good-quality ingredients. Meat can be purchased either fresh or fresh frozen, and carbohydrate can be in the form of home-made biscuits or even pasta. Take advice from your vet when adding vitamins and minerals.

The BARF diet needs careful researching and slight modifying to be suitable for a Bulldog. A popular ingredient is raw chicken wings, which Bulldogs are inclined to swallow whole – with a risk of choking. These should be substituted with minced chicken.

Whatever food you decide on, it is wise to supervise your Bulldog's mealtimes, as they tend to grab their food and swallow it in lumps, which, again, can lead to choking.

PUPPY DIET

The breeder of your Bulldog puppy should carefully explain to you the diet and feeding regime that has been followed, and also supply you with a diet sheet. It is wise to adhere to this diet sheet, as any sudden changes may upset the puppy's stomach. If, for any reason, you have to change the ingredients, it should be done over a period of at least a week or two.

At 10 weeks of age, your Bulldog puppy should be on four meals a day, two milk-based and two meat-based. Between 13 and 16 weeks, one of the milk meals can be dropped; between six months and 12 months, the pup should be fed twice daily.

ADULT DIET

A Bulldog that eats well can have his allocated meal portion divided into two feeds. However, if your dog is not so enthusiastic about his meals, one meal a day is fine. If you are feeding a manufactured food, you need to give the recommended portions with a slight adjustment in relation to your Bulldog's age and activity. Alternatively, if you are feeding a home-made diet, he needs daily approximately 58 kilocalories per kg of bodyweight, which is somewhere in the region of 1,450 g per day if he weighs a typical 25 kgs (55 lbs) based on an assumption of tripe 0.9 kcal/, mixer 3.5 kcal/g and mince 2.0 kcal/g.

Initially, your puppy will need four meals a day.

Remember, as with a pup, an adult Bulldog needs any diet change introduced gradually over a week or so. Bulldogs either live to eat or eat to live, so I would not recommend free feeding – leaving free access to feed at all times. Indeed, I have not known this method to work successfully, but that is not to rule it out completely, as every Bulldog is an individual.

From time to time, there is no reason not to treat your Bulldog with household table scraps, providing they do not contain the following:

- Cooked bone is dangerous and will splinter; the only bone a Bulldog can have is a very large marrow bone, served raw.
- Onions.
- Chocolate in any form or flavouring.
- Grapes and currants/sultanas must be avoided as they can be highly toxic, if not lethal.
- Good-quality pork is fine for most dogs, but some may show sensitivity.

However, some boneless chicken, beef or lamb, served with leftover vegetables and mixed with gravy, will be received and eaten with relish. Other foods that should be avoided are sweets/candy, sweet puddings (except low-sugar rice pudding) and chewing gum, which contains xylitol.

Our own Bulldogs enjoy the occasional piece of bread or toast as a treat.

FADDY FEEDERS

Bulldogs can be faddy feeders. If you have one of these, you must stick to one type of food because if you keep changing, your dog will eat the new food for one day only. Equally, you are advised not to give a faddy feeder delicious treats or he will never return to his mundane daily feed.

If your Bulldog decides not to eat his meal, then take it away from him and serve it again at the next sitting. Do not be alarmed if he refuses food for a couple of days; providing he has fresh water, he won't come to any harm and eventually he will eat, I promise!

MAKING ADJUSTMENTS

As your Bulldog advances in years, you must adjust his calorific intake to suit his less active lifestyle. You may have to divide his food into smaller feeds and, perhaps, tempt him with tasty morsels, although I have to say that our 'oldies' have always enjoyed their food to the last. If you have more than one Bulldog (or another breed), either feed them separately or stand between them, because the faster eater will cast his eye on the other dog's remaining food and it could lead to a disagreement. Bulldogs should never be fed either immediately before or after exercise; leave at least an hour clear each way.

OBESITY

Just like humans, there are some Bulldogs who are 'good doers'. No matter what they eat and how much they exercise, they carry weight. You can bulk these dogs up with empty calories by boiling cabbage and or carrots in meat stock and substituting this for a percentage of their normal diet. In this way, the dog feels full without taking on board calories. Always check with your vet first that your dog has no medical reason why he gains weight – or, for that matter, fails to gain weight.

There is no excuse, indeed it is an act of cruelty, to over-feed and under-exercise a normal, healthy dog and keep him fat.

PREGNANCY

During most of her pregnancy, the expectant mother should be kept on her normal feed and regular daily intake. Just because she is pregnant, there is no excuse to make her fat! From week six of the pregnancy, her total weekly feed allowance can be increased by 10 per cent, but only if she is not already carrying too much weight. It is best to avoid any sort of supplement and give her as little salt/sodium in her diet as possible.

Towards the end of her

You need to adjust the quantity you feed to suit your Bulldog's age and lifestyle.

pregnancy, especially if she is carrying a large litter, she may find it difficult to eat all her feed in one go, so she may be fed little and often, and tempted, if necessary, with cooked chicken breast or good-quality raw steak mince. Once she has whelped, she needs to be fed as much as she asks for, but, again, either little and often or spread between two to four meals per 24 hours, as one huge meal could be very dangerous.

During full lactation she could require up to four times her normal daily maintenance amount. Take advice from your veterinary surgeon before supplementing a lactating bitch with calcium; if she is eating a good-quality diet well, she may not require it.

SPECIAL DIETS

As with humans, there are some dogs, Bulldogs included, who have various dietary intolerances. It is best to take advice from your veterinary surgeon regarding an individual dog's special diet. However, you can make your own, using ingredients like fish and rice. Alternatively, buy a commercially made food, usually through your vet. There are now many different brands available.

OTHER TREATS

Everybody likes a treat, and Bulldogs are no different. As mentioned earlier, they can have suitable household table scraps as a treat, and firm favourites with all Bulldogs are cooked chicken and cheese. There is a wide range of dog treat biscuits you can buy or, indeed, you could make your own. A whole raw carrot can be enjoyed and also helps to clean the teeth, as does a whole raw marrow bone. Slices of apple, melon and banana may be accepted and are healthy treats to give.

Liver, heart or other offal may be given cooked occasionally, but not frequently, as they are too high in certain vitamins. Do not give your Bulldog any dried rawhide chews or other similar dried animal parts, including pig's ears and cattle hooves. The Bulldog's tendency to grab and swallow makes all these items a potential choking hazard and they are even more dangerous when softened with saliva.

If you keep your Bulldog fit and lean, he will live a longer, more active life.

ROUTINE CARE

A daily brush will keep your Bulldog's coat in good order.

Cleaning the wrinkles – and keeping them dry – is an essential task.

Ear cleansing wipes can be used to remove debris from the ears.

ROUTINE CARE

The Bulldog is a low-maintenance breed in terms of coat care, but spending time grooming your Bulldog will help develop a special bond between you as well as keeping him in sparkling condition.

COAT CARE

The Bulldog has a short, smooth coat, which will benefit from a daily brushing with a soft pony 'body brush' followed by a wipe over with a piece of silk cloth to bring out the shine. You can use one of the many spray-on coat conditioners now available as you brush.

As a short-coated breed, a Bulldog will shed hair daily, but at certain times of the year he will have a heavier moult. For removing extra dead hair easily, we find a stripping blade (shaped like a wood saw, bent in half) does a great job. These can be found at most large pet stores. From time to time, your Bulldog will appreciate and, on occasion, require a bath. The easiest way to do this is to place a non-slip rubber mat in the shower cubicle and wash him in there. He must be rinsed clear of all shampoo, and care must be taken to dry him thoroughly – Bulldogs adore being towel dried. From an early

age, we teach our Bulldogs to accept being dried with a hair dryer.

FACE

The wrinkles on the face, which are so much a part of the Bulldog's heritage, must be inspected daily and kept clean and dry. The best plan is to use unscented wipes, dry with cotton-wool, and then apply an antiseptic powder. If the skin appears red or raw, Sudocrem (or a similar nappy-rash cream) can be applied.

Tear stains must be wiped dry daily. The face wrinkles can be kept stain-free by dabbing on a pinch of Boric powder, available

Regular bushing will keep teeth clean and gums healthy.

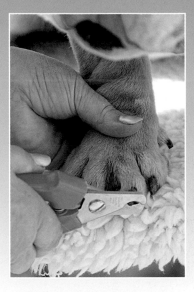

Accustom your Bulldog to nail-trimming from an early age.

from a good, old-fashioned chemist.

EYES
Eyes should be clear and bright. If you have any concerns, they must be referred to your veterinary surgeon immediately. The earlier a vet deals with an eye problem, the least chance of long-term damage.

EARS
Ears should also be inspected on a daily basis and any debris should be gently removed with special ear-cleansing wipes, or you can use cotton-wool. Take care not to dig into the ear canal, especially with cotton buds. Again, if you have any concerns, consult your vet.

TEETH
Teach your Bulldog from an early age to accept having his teeth brushed with a soft toothbrush. This, along with a good diet with some crunchy foods in it (hard kibble, dog biscuits or carrots), should be enough to keep his teeth and gums clean and healthy. A build-up of tartar can damage your dog's internal organs, so regular cleaning is essential.

FEET
For his health and comfort, a Bulldog's nails must be kept short. An adult Bulldog with a good foot shape and who gets proper exercise should never need his nails trimmed except for his dew claws. However, it is well worth getting your Bulldog accustomed to nail-clippers from an early age, as it is so much easier to trim nails on a compliant dog as opposed to a squirming one! You could also file your Bulldog's nails using a large file from a DIY store or using an electric nail file.

When clipping or filing, take care not to nick the quick of the nail, as this hurts the dog and causes bleeding. Your local canine beautician/grooming parlour or, indeed, your vet will help you with any concerns you may have regarding nails.

Some strains of Bulldog are prone to inter-digital cysts between their toes, notably on the front feet but sometimes on the back. These start off as a small, red swelling, which the Bulldog may worry or lick. If you inspect your Bulldog's feet daily, you will spot any signs of trouble at an early stage. The best course of action is to apply lime juice, either from a fresh lime or the type that is sold on home-baking

aisles at supermarkets. If you do this two to three times during the day, the cyst will quickly disappear. We do not know how or why this works – it just does!

If you have missed the initial signs and the cyst develops to fruition, try submersing the foot in warm, salt water for several minutes twice daily. This will help to draw the cyst and reduce the swelling and pain. Inter-digital cysts are basically harmless and do not last long, but if they repeatedly re-occur in the same spot, they can leave a permanent and unsightly lump.

TAIL
The Bulldog is an undocked breed and every one of them has an individual tail, in both length and shape. The tail should also be inspected daily at the root, and kept clear of irritating dead hair where applicable. If necessary, a weekly smear of nappy rash cream can keep tight tail areas free from problems.

EXERCISE
Although not suitable for overland hiking, many misguided folk obtain a Bulldog thinking that this is a dog that does not

A youngster will get as much exercise as he needs playing in the garden.

A Bulldog who has regular exercise will build up a fair degree of fitness and stamina.

require any exercise. In reality, the Bulldog that is kept in fit, hard, condition will almost certainly live a longer, healthier, and more active life. As well as the physical benefits, exercise is important for any dog for his mental well-being.

PUPPIES

Exercise for puppies under 12 months should be limited to their own form of exercise, i.e. playing at their own pace and several very short walks to get them used to being on a collar and lead. Excessive exercise on pups under 12 months of age can lead to damaged joints and bone distortion.

For general socialisation, which involves meeting other people, being exposed to traffic and other situations, you can take your puppy in the car to your local supermarket or market. Find a bench and sit outside for a while so your Bulldog has a chance to take it all in. *For more information, see Chapter Six: Training and Socialisation.*

A Bulldog pup loves to run and play, and this form of exercise gives his body the chance to develop naturally, providing he also has the opportunity to rest at frequent intervals, which is equally important. On summer days, the play area must be shaded.

ADULTS

Overweight, unfit humans have trouble breathing, and Bulldogs are no different. An adult Bulldog should have regular daily walks, to keep him muscled and toned, and to keep his circulatory system in good order. Walking on a hard surface will also help to keep his nails short. Two shorter walks of 20 to 30 minutes are preferable to one long outing. Work him up to this amount of exercise gradually, starting with 10 to 15 minutes per walk.

Ideally, walks should be divided between times when your Bulldog walks beside you on a lead, and free-running in a safe environment. When near livestock, however, your Bulldog must be kept on a lead at all times – the old instincts still exist, and Bulldogs will give cattle in particular a speculative look. Apart from the fact that a farmer has every right to shoot dogs that harass livestock, excited cattle can easily knock down fences and trample dogs and their

Swimming is a great form of exercise, and you know your Bulldog will be safe if you use the services of a hydrotherapy pool.

owners. If you are in an area where there is livestock, make sure you put your Bulldog on a lead in good time – it is surprising just how fast and how far he can travel when the mood takes him!

Although some Bulldogs love water and can swim, many do not take to this form of exercise. Keep your Bulldog on a lead if you are near deep ponds, fast-flowing rivers, or beaches that shelve deeply away or have strong currents. Swimming pools are particularly lethal and must be securely fenced in.

If you wish to use water as a form of exercise for your Bulldog, choose a canine hydrotherapy pool recommended by your vet with fully qualified staff. As the Bulldog has a heavy head, he tends to be top-heavy and may need floats to balance him. An

alternative to the pool is a treadmill situated in a chest-depth amount of water, again to be found at canine hydrotherapy centres. If your Bulldog really hates water, do not force the issue, as this breed is prone to lethal stress in certain situations.

Finally, Bulldogs must not be walked or allowed to free exercise during the day when the temperatures are high. In the summer months and in hot climates, exercise must be conducted in very early morning or late evening. If you live in a humid climate, seek advice from an experienced local vet.

PLAYTIME
Bulldogs have a tremendous sense of humour and love to play, whether retrieving an article, playing hide-and-seek, being dressed up by the kids, or chasing butterflies! There are a

whole host of canine educational toys on the market whereby the dog has to work out how to extract a treat from a toy. For retrieving games, use either a soft gundog 'dummy' or one of the large, soft rope toys. Teach your Bulldog to come back to you and release the article immediately.

Tug-of-war games are not necessarily a good idea, as they can teach bad habits. I am not an advocate of dogs playing with balls, but the best I have found is the type that resembles a string vest but will still bounce. It is difficult for a dog to swallow this type of ball, and the shape allows for easy breathing when it is being retrieved. Never allow your Bulldog to play with a ball that is small enough for him to swallow, or which might get stuck in his throat, and never allow him to play with sticks or stones.

The Bulldog has a unique sense of humour and thoroughly enjoys a game of dressing-up!

If the weather is inclement, why not teach your Bulldog to search for hidden treats around the house? Let him watch you hide the treat the first couple of times – he will soon catch on. Bulldogs are happy to play with each other or indeed other pets. However, they can be very jealous over toys and articles, so our Bulldogs play with each other, but with no toys present.

THE OLDER BULLDOG

The older Bulldog's needs are slightly different from his younger kennelmates'. He has given a lifetime of love and companionship, so the least he can expect is a comfortable old age.

He will need lots of clean, soft, comfortable bedding, and his bed should be placed well away from draughts. It is very important not

to let your elderly Bulldog put on too much weight. In our experience, as a Bulldog gets older he can appear to get increasingly hungry, and the temptation is to let him eat his fill. This, coupled with an older Bulldog's natural need for less exercise, can result in gross obesity – which, in turn, will result in an early death

If your elderly Bulldog seems to

Be aware of your Bulldog's changing needs as he grows older.

be craving food, we find that filling him up with cooked vegetables does the trick, in as much as it fills him up without putting on any weight.

Once a Bulldog gets into his later years, a short amble around the garden, two or three times a day, is probably all he will want or need. We are fortunate to have a large field next to our property. The youngsters are walked around the perimeter, while our oldies come part way and then wait for our return before coming back into the yard.

LETTING GO
Sooner or later, you will be faced with the difficult decision as to whether the time has come to put your much-loved pet to sleep. This decision, although always hard, is one that should never be shirked. It is the last show of true love that you can give your Bulldog in his time of need. The temptation to keep him alive for selfish reasons must always be resisted. Once his quality of life has diminished to such an extent that he can no

THE BEST OF CARE

longer get about without being in pain, or he has stopped eating, then the most loving thing you can do is to end his life peacefully and with dignity.

If you are very lucky, your Bulldog will pass away in his sleep. If this is not to be, then you should be guided by your vet. On the few occasions we have had to do this, we have made an appointment at the end of surgery or, if necessary, we have arranged for the vet to come to us. For those who have never

seen a dog put to sleep, I can say that although it is distressing, it is the last and probably the most rewarding thing that you can do for your beloved pet. It just involves a painless injection, which is quickly followed by sleep before passing away.

Your vet will advise you about local pet crematoria and the staff will talk you through all the options available. Should you not want this, your vet will arrange for the cremation to be carried out.

Although, at the time, you will feel completely devastated at losing a loyal family friend, the old saying that time is a great healer is true. I am sure that, in time, with the help of photos or videos to watch, you will be able to recall all the happy times spent with your Bulldog. A much-loved pet should never be forgotten, but when the time is right, you may think of getting another pup, who will once again bring laughter and love into your life.

In time you will be able to look back and remember all the happy times you spent with your beloved Bulldog.

TRAINING AND SOCIALISATION

Chapter 6

When you decided to bring a Bulldog into your life, you probably had dreams of how it was going to be with this very special member of the canine race. You may have envisaged rambles with your Bulldog ambling along beside, you, cosy evenings with your Bulldog lying devotedly at your feet, and, whenever you returned home, there would always be a special welcome waiting for you.

There is no doubt that you can achieve all this and much more with a Bulldog, but like anything that is worth having, you must be prepared to put in the work. A Bulldog, regardless of whether he is a puppy or an adult, does not come ready trained, understanding exactly what you want and fitting perfectly into your lifestyle. He has to learn his place in your family and he must discover what is acceptable behaviour.

We have a great starting point in that the breed has an outstanding temperament. This is a dog that is naturally gregarious, and loves being surrounded by people. He is loyal and affectionate, and is generally eager to please. It is your job to bring out the best in him.

THE FAMILY PACK

Dogs have been domesticated for some 14,000 years, but luckily for us, they have inherited and retained behaviour from their distant ancestor – the wolf. A Bulldog may never have lived in the wild, but he is born with the survival skills and the mentality of a meat-eating predator who hunts in a pack. A wolf living in a pack owes its existence to mutual co-operation and an acceptance of a hierarchy, as this ensures both food and protection. A domesticated dog living in a family pack has exactly the same outlook. He wants food, companionship, and leadership – and it is your job to provide for these needs.

YOUR ROLE

Theories about dog behaviour and methods of training go in and out of fashion, but in reality, nothing has changed from the day when wolves ventured in from the wild to join the family circle. The wolf (and equally the dog) accepts a subservient place in the family pack in return for food and protection. In a dog's eyes, you are his leader and he relies on you to make all the important decisions. This does not mean that you have to act like a dictator or a bully. You are accepted as a leader, without argument, as long as you have the right credentials.

Have you got what it takes to be a firm, fair and consistent leader?

you may think you don't have to take this on board for a few months, but that would be a big mistake. With a Bulldog you need to start as you mean to go on. Bulldog pups are remarkably cute – and they know it! A Bulldog puppy can be manipulative, and you may find that bad habits picked up in puppyhood can be very difficult to rectify.

When your Bulldog first arrives in his new home, follow these guidelines:

- **Keep it simple:** Decide on the rules you want your Bulldog to obey and always make it 100 per cent clear what is acceptable, and what is unacceptable, behaviour.

- **Be consistent:** If you are not consistent about enforcing rules, how can you expect your Bulldog to take you seriously? There is nothing worse than allowing your Bulldog to jump on the sofa one moment and then scolding him the next time he does it because he is muddy. As far as the Bulldog is concerned, he may as well try it on because he can't predict your reaction. Bear in mind, inconsistency leads to insecurity.

- **Get your timing right:** If you are rewarding your Bulldog – and equally if you are reprimanding him – you must respond within one to two seconds otherwise the dog will not link his behaviour with your reaction (see page 84).

- **Read your dog's body language:** Find out how to

The first part of the job is easy. You are the provider and you are therefore respected because you supply food. In a Bulldog's eyes, you must be the ultimate hunter, because a day never goes by when you cannot find food. The second part of the leader's job description is straightforward, but for some reason we find it hard to achieve. In order for a dog to accept his place in the family pack, he must respect his leader as the decision-maker. A low-ranking pack animal does not question authority; he is perfectly happy to see someone else shoulder the responsibility. Problems will only arise if you cut a poor figure as leader and the dog feels he should mount a challenge for the top-ranking role.

HOW TO BE A GOOD LEADER

There are a number of guidelines to follow to establish yourself in the role of leader in a way that your Bulldog understands and respects. If you have a puppy, read body language and facial expressions (see page 82) so that you understand your Bulldog's feelings and intentions. This can be tricky with a Bulldog, but once you are in tune with him, you will be able to pick up minor changes in expression and body posture.

- **Be aware of your own body language:** When you ask your Bulldog to do something, do not 'eyeball' him or he will think you are being confrontational. Keep your manner bright and breezy, which will invite his co-operation. You can also help your dog to learn by using your body language to communicate with him. For example, if you want your dog to come to you, open your arms out and look inviting. If you want your dog to stay, use a hand signal (palm flat, facing the dog) so you are effectively 'blocking' his advance.

- **Tone of voice:** Dogs do not speak English; they learn by associating a word with the required action. However, they are very receptive to tone of voice, so you can use your voice to praise him or to correct undesirable behaviour. If you are pleased with your Bulldog, praise him to the skies in a warm, happy voice. If you want to stop him raiding the bin, use a deep, stern voice when you say "No".

- **Give one command only:** If you keep repeating a command, or keep

A Bulldog is very clever at tuning into his human family.

changing it, your Bulldog will think you are babbling and will probably ignore you. If your Bulldog does not respond the first time you ask, make it simple by using a treat to lure him into position and then you can reward him for a correct response.

- **Daily reminders:** A young Bulldog is apt to forget his manners from time to time and an adolescent dog may attempt to challenge your authority (see page 96). Rather than coming

down on your Bulldog like a ton of bricks when he does something wrong, try to prevent bad manners by daily reminders of good manners. For example:

i. Do not let your dog barge ahead of you when you are going through a door.

ii Do not let him leap out of the car the moment you open the door (which could be potentially lethal, as well as being disrespectful).

iii. Do not let him eat from

MEETING AND GREETING

If you observe two dogs meeting each other, you will learn a lot about canine body language.

Both dogs are upright in posture and appear tense as they first make contact.

Within seconds, the body language changes as both dogs relax, sensing that the intentions on both sides are friendly rather than threatening.

your hand when you are at the table.

iv. Do not let him 'win' a toy at the end of a play session and then make off with it. You 'own' his toys and you 'allow' him to play with them. Your Bulldog must learn to give up a toy when you ask.

UNDERSTANDING YOUR BULLDOG

Body language is an important means of communication between dogs, which they use to make friends, to assert status and to avoid conflict. It is important to get on your dog's wavelength by understanding his body language and reading his facial expressions.

- A positive body posture, with head held upright and ears back, indicates a happy, confident dog. A Bulldog does not always have a tail to wag – but he will certainly show when he is feeling happy. Those with tails wag them; those without tails wag their whole back end. A Bulldog will also laugh – literally panting with a big, wide grin on his face.
- A crouched body posture with the head turning to one side and a pained expression shows that a dog is being submissive. A dog may do this when he is being told off or if a more assertive dog approaches him.
- A bold dog will stand tall, looking strong and alert. His ears will be as forward as they can be, and his expression will be keen and alert.
- A dog who raises his hackles (lifting the fur along his

topline) is trying to look as scary as possible.

- A playful dog will go down on his front legs while standing on his hind legs in a bow position. This friendly invitation says: "I'm no threat, let's play."
- A dominant, aggressive dog will meet other dogs with a hard stare if he is challenged. His ears will be as forward as they can be, and he will appear tense in every muscle. Bulldogs do not bare their teeth (their thick chops prevent this) and many do not growl. If a Bulldog does growl, he will lower his head to the floor, which was a way of protecting his head from bulls. A Bulldog prefers the 'menace stare,' approaching with his neck arched stallion-like, and walking on tip toes.
- A nervous dog will often show aggressive behaviour as a means of self-protection. Nervous Bulldogs either curl up and 'die', or bite without prior warning.
- Bulldogs very, very rarely challenge humans in an aggressive way. If it ever happens, it is because the Bulldog is either ill, sick, or injured (or has suffered cruelty previously). A dominant Bulldog will keep thrusting his head into you, or between you and whatever takes your attention away from him. A typical sign of dominance in both males and females is 'riding' (or mating), as in adopting a sexual behaviour pattern.

- If a Bulldog wishes to retain a toy or guard it, he will lower his head on it and stare very calmly at you – he could still be wagging his tail.

Two Bulldogs about to fight will lower their heads and stare at each other through hooded lids; there is no warning sound before fighting starts. They generally make a lot of unusual noises (grunting and snorting), which other breeds of dog interpret as aggressive behaviour, then pile in. Once attacked, the Bulldog will fight to the death. Once a Bulldog has fallen out with another dog or individual, he will never, ever forgive.

GIVING REWARDS

Why should your Bulldog do as you ask? If you follow the guidelines given above, your Bulldog should respect your authority, but what about the time when he has just met a dog in the park or has found a really enticing scent? The answer is that you must always be the most interesting, the most attractive and the most irresistible person in your Bulldog's eyes. It would be nice to think that you could achieve this by personality alone, but most of us need a little extra help. You need to find out what is the biggest reward for your dog. In most cases, a Bulldog will be motivated to work for food

TOP TREATS

Some trainers grade treats depending on what they are asking the dog to do. A dog may get a low-grade treat (such as a piece of dry food) to reward good behaviour on a random basis, such as sitting when you open a door or allowing you to examine his teeth. High-grade treats (which may be cooked liver, sausage or cheese) may be reserved for training new exercises, or for use in the park when you want a really good recall, for example.

Whatever type of treat you use, you should remember to subtract it from your Bulldog's daily food ration. Bulldogs are prone to obesity. Fat dogs are lethargic, prone to health problems and will almost certainly have a shorter life expectancy, so reward your Bulldog, but always keep a check on his figure!

For some Bulldogs a game with a toy is the biggest reward.

reward, although some prefer a game with a toy. This could be a ragger, a ball, or a gundog dummy. But whatever reward you use, make sure it is something that your dog really wants.

When you are teaching a dog a new exercise, you should reward your Bulldog frequently. When he knows the exercise or command, reward him randomly so that he keeps on responding to you in a positive manner.

If your Bulldog does something extra special, like coming back to you the moment you call him, make sure he really knows how pleased you are by giving him lots of verbal praise or his favourite treat. If he gets a bonanza reward, he is more likely to come back on future occasions because you have proved to be even more rewarding than his previous activity. Bulldogs love praise and being stroked more than any other reward!

HOW DO DOGS LEARN?
It is not difficult to get inside your Bulldog's head and understand how he learns, as it is not dissimilar to the way we learn. Dogs learn by conditioning: they find out that specific behaviours produce specific consequences. This is known as operant conditioning or consequence learning. Consequences have to be immediate or clearly linked to the behaviour, as a dog sees the world in terms of action and result. Dogs will quickly learn if an action has a bad consequence or a good consequence.

Dogs also learn by association. This is known as classical conditioning or association learning. It is the type of learning made famous by Pavlov's experiment with dogs. Pavlov presented dogs with food and measured their salivary response (how much they drooled). Then he rang a bell just before presenting the food. At first, the dogs did not salivate until the food was presented. But after a while they learnt that the sound of the bell meant that food was coming and so they salivated when they heard the bell. A dog needs to learn the association in order for it to have any meaning. For example, a dog that has never seen a lead before will be completely indifferent to it. A dog that has learnt that a lead means he is going for a walk will get excited the second he sees the lead; he has learnt to associate a lead with a walk.

BE POSITIVE
The most effective method of training dogs is to use their ability to learn by consequence and to teach that the behaviour you want produces a good consequence. For example, if you ask your Bulldog to "Sit" and

reward him with a treat when he does so, he will learn that it is worth his while to sit on command because it will lead to a treat. He is far more likely to repeat the behaviour and the behaviour will become stronger, because it results in a positive outcome. This method of training is known as positive reinforcement and it generally leads to a happy, co-operative dog that is willing to work and a handler who has fun training their dog.

The opposite approach is negative reinforcement. This is far less effective and often results in a poor relationship between dog and owner. In this method of training, you ask your Bulldog to "Sit" and if he does not respond, you deliver a sharp yank on the training collar or push his rear to the ground. The dog learns that not responding to your command has a bad consequence and he may be less likely to ignore you in the future. However, it may well have a bad consequence for you, too. A dog that is treated in this way may associate harsh handling with the handler and become aggressive or fearful. Instead of establishing a pattern of willing co-operation, you are establishing a relationship built on coercion. A Bulldog who is harshly handled and forced to do things he does not want to do will go into stress shock, which can cause death in extreme cases.

GETTING STARTED
When you train your Bulldog you will develop your own techniques as you get to know what motivates him. You may decide to get involved with clicker training or you may prefer to go for a simple command-and-reward formula. It does not matter what form of training you use, as long as it is based on positive, reward-based methods.

There are a few important guidelines to bear in mind when

THE CLICKER REVOLUTION

Karen Pryor pioneered the technique of clicker training when she was working with dolphins. It is very much a continuation of Pavlov's work and makes full use of association learning. Karen wanted to mark 'correct' behaviour at the precise moment it happened. She found it was impossible to toss a fish to a dolphin when it was in mid-air, when she wanted to reward it. Her aim was to establish a conditioned response so the dolphin knew that it had performed correctly and a reward would follow.

The solution was the clicker: a small matchbox-shaped training aid, with a metal tongue that makes a click when it is pressed. To begin with, the dolphin had to learn that a click meant that food was coming. The dolphin then learnt that it must 'earn' a click in order to get a reward. Clicker training has been used with many different animals, most particularly with dogs, and it has proved hugely successful. It is a great aid for pet owners and is also widely used by professional trainers who are teach highly specialised skills.

Make training fun so your Bulldog wants to co-operate with you.

you are training your Bulldog:
- Find a training area that is free from distractions, particularly when you are just starting out. The Bulldog can be quite a nosey, inquisitive dog, and he may prefer to check out his surrounding rather than concentrate on his lessons.
- Keep training sessions short, especially with young puppies that have very short attention spans. Remember, the Bulldog

is not a breed with a strong working instinct, and he will become bored by monotony and repetition.
- Do not train if you are in a bad mood or if you are on a tight schedule – the training session will be doomed to failure.
- If you are using a toy as a reward, make sure it is only available when you are training. In this way it has an added value for your Bulldog.

- If you are using food treats, make sure they are bite-size and easy to swallow; you don't want to hang about while your Bulldog chews on his treat.
- Do not attempt to train your Bulldog after he has eaten, or soon after returning from exercise. He will either be too full up to care about food treats or too tired to concentrate.
- When you are training, move around your allocated area so that your dog does not think that an exercise can only be performed in one place.
- If your Bulldog is finding an exercise difficult, try not to get frustrated. Go back a step and praise him for his effort. You will probably find he is more successful when you try again at the next training session.
- If a training session is not going well – either because you are in the wrong frame of mind or the dog is not focusing – ask your Bulldog to do something you know he can do (such as a trick he enjoys performing) and then you can reward him with a food treat or a play with his favourite toy, ending the session on a happy, positive note.
- Do not train for too long. You need to end a training session on a high, with your Bulldog wanting more, rather than making him sour by asking too much of him.

In the exercises that follow, clicker training is introduced and followed, but all the exercises will work without the use of a clicker.

INTRODUCING A CLICKER

This is dead easy, and the intelligent Bulldog will learn about the clicker in record time! It can be combined with attention training, which is a very useful tool and can be used on many different occasions.

- Prepare some treats and go to an area that is free from distractions. Allow your Bulldog to wander and when he stops to look at you, click and reward by throwing him a treat. This means he will not crowd you, but will go looking for the treat. Repeat a couple of times. If your Bulldog is very easily distracted, you may need to start this exercise with the dog on a lead.
- After a few clicks, your Bulldog will understand that if he hears a click, he will get a treat. He must now learn that he must 'earn' a click. This time, when your Bulldog looks at you, wait a little longer before clicking and then reward him. If your Bulldog is on a lead but responding well, try him off the lead.
- When your Bulldog is working for a click and giving you his attention, you can introduce a cue or command word, such as "Watch". Repeat a few times, using the cue. You now have a Bulldog that understands the clicker and will give you his attention when you ask him to "Watch".

TRAINING EXERCISES

When you are training your Bulldog, play to his strengths. He does not have the lightning-fast brain of a Border Collie, for example, but when he learns something, it remains firmly instilled. Be patient, and be generous with your rewards and with your praise so that your Bulldog knows he is pleasing you. A Bulldog is a 'thinking' breed and likes to work out the pros and cons of a situation. He will decide if co-operating with you is a good idea, so make sure you keep training sessions light-hearted and full of fun so he decides that being with you and co-operating with you is to his advantage.

Never be confrontational. If your Bulldog is struggling with an exercise, or seems to be acting dumb, simply ask him to do something different. This could be a trick that he will enjoy performing, or something easy, like a Sit, so you can reward your Bulldog for co-operating. *Never* resort to harsh handling. This applies to training dogs of all breeds, but most especially to a Bulldog who will become stubborn and resentful.

With practice, you can phase out the lure and your Bulldog will "Sit" on cue.

Teaching the Down may take some patience so, in the early stages, reward any movement to go into the correct position.

THE SIT

This is the easiest exercise to teach, so it is rewarding for both you and your Bulldog.

- Choose a tasty treat and hold it just above your puppy's nose. As he looks up at the treat, he will naturally go into the 'Sit'. As soon as he is in position, reward him.
- Repeat the exercise and when your pup understands what you want, introduce the "Sit" command.
- You can practise the Sit exercise at mealtimes by holding out the bowl and waiting for your dog to sit. Most Bulldogs learn this one very quickly!

THE DOWN

This can be a difficult exercise to teach, as a Bulldog may feel vulnerable when he is in the Down position, and may even panic. Take this exercise slowly and reward frequently.

- You can start with your dog in a 'Sit', or it is just as effective to teach it when the dog is standing. Hold a treat just below your puppy's nose and slowly lower it towards the ground. The treat acts as a lure and your puppy will follow it, first going down on his forequarters and then bringing his hindquarters down as he tries to get the treat.
- Make sure you close your fist around the treat and only reward your puppy with the treat when he is in the correct position. If your puppy is reluctant to go 'Down', you can apply gentle pressure on his shoulders to encourage him to go into the correct position.
- When your puppy is following the treat and going into position, introduce a verbal command.
- Build up this exercise over a period of time, each time waiting a little longer before giving the reward, so the puppy learns to stay in the 'Down' position. A Bulldog will panic if he is placed 'upside down' on his back, so this should be avoided at all costs.

You can start to build a response to the Recall with your Bulldog on the lead.

The aim is to build up a positive response so your Bulldog can be called away from distractions.

THE RECALL

All dogs are individuals, and this is particularly true of Bulldogs. Some Bulldogs are happy to stroll beside you off-lead, and will respond to the recall reasonably promptly. However, there are other Bulldogs who go completely 'deaf' if something attracts their attention, and some may even try to chase livestock, given the opportunity.

The best chance of success is to start training when your Bulldog is very young and is still feeling insecure. This will give him the incentive to stay with you and not stray too far afield. Hopefully, the breeder will have already started recall training by calling the puppies in from outside and rewarding them with some treats scattered on the floor. But even if this has not been the case, you will find that a puppy arriving in his new home is highly responsive. His chief desire is to follow you and be with you. Capitalise on this from day one by getting your pup's attention and calling him to you in a bright, excited tone of voice.

• Practise in the garden. When your puppy is busy exploring, get his attention by calling his name, and, as he runs towards you, introduce the verbal command "Come". Make sure you sound happy and exciting, so your puppy wants to come to you. When he responds, give him lots of praise.

• If your puppy is slow to respond, try running away a few paces or jumping up and down. It doesn't matter how silly you look, the key issue is to get your puppy's attention and then make yourself irresistible!

• In a dog's mind, coming when called should be regarded as the best fun because he knows he is always going to be rewarded. Never make the mistake of telling your dog off, no matter how slow he is to respond, as you will undo all your previous hard work.

• When you are free running your dog, make sure you have his favourite toy or a pocket full of treats so you can reward

SECRET WEAPON

You can build up a strong recall by using another form of association learning. Buy a whistle and when you are giving your Bulldog his food, peep on the whistle. You can choose the type of signal you want to give: two short peeps or one long whistle, for example. Within a matter of days, your dog will learn that the sound of the whistle means that food is coming.

Now transfer the lesson outside. Arm yourself with some tasty treats and the whistle. Allow your Bulldog to run free in the garden, and, after a couple of minutes, use the whistle. The dog has already learnt to associate the whistle with food, so he will come towards you.

Immediately reward him with a treat and lots of praise. Repeat the lesson a few times in the garden, so you are confident that your dog is responding before trying it in the park. Make sure you always have some treats in your pocket when you go for a walk and your dog will quickly learn how rewarding it is to come to you.

him at intervals throughout the walk when you call him to you. Do not allow your dog to run free and only call him back at the end of the walk to clip on his lead. An intelligent Bulldog will soon realise that the recall means the end of his walk and then end of fun – so who can blame him for not wanting to come back?

TRAINING LINE
This is the equivalent of a very long lead, which you can buy at a pet store, or you can make your own with a length of rope. The training line is attached to your Bulldog's collar and should be around 15 feet (4.5 metres) in length.

The purpose of the training line

is to prevent your Bulldog from disobeying you so that he never has the chance to get into bad habits. For example, when you call your Bulldog and he ignores you, you can immediately pick up the end of the training line and call him again. By picking up the line you will have attracted his attention and if you call in an excited, happy voice, your Bulldog will come to you. The moment he reaches you, give him a tasty treat so he is instantly rewarded for making the 'right' decision.

The training line is very useful when your Bulldog becomes an adolescent and is testing your leadership. When you have reinforced the correct behaviour a number of times, your dog will

build up a strong recall and you will not need to use a training line.

WALKING ON A LOOSE LEAD
This is a simple exercise, which baffles many Bulldog owners. The Bulldog is a very strong dog, and if he gets into the habit of setting his shoulders and pulling on the lead, every outing will be a misery. In most cases, owners make the mistake of wanting to get on with the expedition rather that training the dog how to walk on a lead.

In this exercise, as with all lessons that you teach your Bulldog, you must adopt a calm, determined, no-nonsense attitude so he knows that you mean business. Once your Bulldog is

You want your Bulldog to walk beside you on a loose lead, neither pulling ahead nor lagging behind.

Use a hand signal and a verbal cue to teach your Bulldog to "Stay".

prepared to take you seriously, he will be ready to co-operate with you.

- In the early stages of lead training, allow your puppy to pick his route and follow him. He will get used to the feeling of being 'attached' to you and has no reason to put up any resistance.
- Next, find a toy or a tasty treat and show it to your puppy. Let him follow the treat/toy for a few paces and then reward him.
- Build up the amount of time your pup will walk with you, and, when he is walking nicely by your side, introduce the verbal command "Heel" or "Close". Give lots of praise when your pup is in the

correct position.
- When your pup is walking alongside you, keep focusing his attention on you by using his name and then rewarding him when he looks at you. If it is going well, introduce some changes of direction.
- Do not attempt to take your puppy out on the lead until you have mastered the basics at home. You need to be confident that your puppy accepts the lead and will focus his attention on you, when requested, before you face the challenge of a busy environment.
- If you are heading somewhere special, such as the park, your Bulldog will probably try to pull because he is impatient to

get there. If this happens, stop, call your dog to you and do not set off again until he is in the correct position. It may take time, but your Bulldog will eventually realise that it is more productive to walk by your side than to pull ahead.

STAYS

This is a useful exercise to teach, but it does not come naturally to Bulldogs, particularly if you are asking for a Down Stay. As with teaching the Down, a Bulldog tends to feel vulnerable if he is left, particularly if he is in the presence of other people or other dogs. However, there are many occasions when you want your Bulldog to stay in position, even if it is only for a few seconds. The classic example is when you want your Bulldog to stay in the back of the car until you have clipped on his lead. Therefore, the best plan is to teach a "Stay" or "Wait" which is of short duration, but is still effective. In this way you can control your Bulldog, but you are not putting him under stress.

Some trainers use the verbal command "Stay" when the dog is to stay in position for an extended period of time and "Wait" if the dog is to stay in position for a few seconds until you give the next command. Others trainers use a universal "Stay" to cover all situations.

- Put your puppy in a 'Sit' or a 'Down' and use a hand signal (flat palm, facing the dog) to show he is to stay in position. Step a pace away from the dog. Wait a second, step back and reward him. If you have a lively pup, you may find it easier to train this exercise on the lead.

- Repeat the exercise, gradually increasing the distance you can leave your dog. When you return to your dog's side, praise him quietly and release him with a command, such as "OK".
- Remember to keep your body language very still when you are training this exercise and avoid eye contact with your dog. Work on this exercise over a period of time and you will build up a really reliable 'Stay'.

SOCIALISATION

While your Bulldog is mastering basic obedience exercises, there is other, equally important work to do with him. A Bulldog is not only becoming a part of your home and family, he is becoming a member of the community. He needs to be able to live in the outside world, coping calmly with every new situation that comes his way. It is your job to introduce him to as many

different experiences as possible and to encourage him to behave in an appropriate manner.

It is also essential that he learns good manners around other dogs. This is important with all breeds, but it is especially important with a Bulldog, who can struggle when interacting with other dogs. This is largely due to the fact that other dogs are not good at reading a Bulldog's facial expressions and body language and may become assertive, prompted by fear or uncertainty. It is also important to remember that the Bulldog was bred to be a fighting dog. This instinct is very much diluted in the modern dog, but a Bulldog that feels threatened will certainly look after himself, which could have grievous consequences. The more work you put in socialising your Bulldog with other dogs of sound temperament, the more likely he is to learn good canine manners.

In order to socialise your

A puppy learns from interacting with his mother and his littermates.

Bulldog effectively, it is helpful to understand how his brain is developing and then you will get a perspective on how he sees the world.

CANINE SOCIALISATION
(Birth to 7 weeks)
This is the time when a dog learns how to be a dog. By interacting with his mother and his littermates, a young pup learns about leadership and submission. He learns to read body posture so that he understands the intentions of his mother and his siblings. A puppy that is taken away from his litter too early may always have behavioural problems with other dogs, either being fearful or aggressive.

SOCIALISATION PERIOD
(7 to 12 weeks)
This is the time to get cracking and introduce your Bulldog puppy to as many different experiences as possible. This includes meeting different people, other dogs and animals, seeing new sights and hearing a range of sounds, from the vacuum cleaner to the roar of traffic. It may be that your Bulldog has been reared in kennels and if this is the case, you must work even harder at this stage of his education. A puppy learns very quickly and what he learns will stay with him for the rest of his life. This is the best time for a puppy to move to a new home, as he is adaptable and ready to form deep bonds.

FEAR-IMPRINT PERIOD
(8 to 11 weeks)
This occurs during the socialisation period and it can be the cause of problems if it is not handled carefully. If a pup is exposed to a frightening or painful experience, it will lead to lasting impressions. Obviously, you will attempt to avoid frightening situations, such as your pup being bullied by a mean-spirited older dog, or a

firework going off, but you cannot always protect your puppy from the unexpected. If your pup has a nasty experience, the best plan is to make light of it and distract him by offering him a treat or a game. The pup will take the lead from you and will be reassured that there is nothing to worry about. If you mollycoddle him and sympathise with him, he is far more likely to retain the memory of his fear.

If a young Bulldog appears apprehensive, give lots of reassurance so he knows there is nothing to fear.

SENIORITY PERIOD
(12 to 16 weeks)

During this period, your Bulldog puppy starts to cut the apron strings and becomes more independent. He will test out his status to find out who is the pack leader: him or you. Bad habits, such as play biting, which may have been seen as endearing a few weeks earlier, should be firmly discouraged. Remember to use positive, reward-based training, but make sure your puppy knows that you are the leader and must be respected.

SECOND FEAR-IMPRINT PERIOD (6 to 14 months)

This period is not as critical as the first fear-imprint period, but it should still be handled carefully. During this time your Bulldog may appear apprehensive, or he may show fear of something familiar. You may feel as if you have taken a backwards step, but if you adopt a calm, positive manner, your Bulldog will see

that there is nothing to be frightened of. Do not make your dog confront the thing that frightens him. Simply distract his attention, and give him something else to think about, such as obeying a simple command, such as "Sit" or "Down". This will give you the opportunity to praise and reward your dog and will help to boost his confidence.

YOUNG ADULTHOOD AND MATURITY (1 to 4 years)

The timing of this phase depends on the size of the dog: the bigger the dog, the later it is. This period coincides with a dog's increased size and strength, mental as well as physical. Some dogs, particularly those with a dominant nature, will test your leadership again and may become aggressive towards other dogs. Firmness and continued training are essential at this time, so that your Bulldog accepts his status in the family pack.

IDEAS FOR SOCIALISATION

When you are socialising your Bulldog, you want him to experience as many different situations as possible. Try out some of the following ideas, which will ensure your Bulldog has an all-round education.

If you are taking on a rescued dog and have little knowledge of his background, it is important to work through a programme of socialisation. A young puppy soaks up new experiences like a sponge, but an older dog can still learn. If a rescued dog shows fear or apprehension, treat him in exactly the same way as you would treat a youngster who is going through the second fear-imprint period.

- Accustom your puppy to household noises, such as the vacuum cleaner, the television and the washing machine.
- Ask visitors to come to the door, wearing different types of clothing – for example, wearing a hat, a long raincoat,

Allow your Bulldog to experience a variety of situations so he learns to react calmly and with confidence.

TRAINING CLUBS

There are lots of training clubs to choose from. Your vet will probably have details of clubs in your area, or you can ask friends who have dogs if they attend a club. Alternatively, use the internet to find out more information. But how do you know if the club is any good?

Before you take your dog, ask if you can go to a class as an observer and find out the following:

- What experience does the instructor(s) have?
- Do they have experience with Bulldogs or any of the Bull breeds?
- Is the class well organised and are the dogs reasonably quiet? (A noisy class indicates an unruly atmosphere, which will not be conducive to learning.)
- Are there are a number of classes to suit dogs of different ages and abilities?
- Are positive, reward-based training methods used?
- Does the club train for the Good Citizen Scheme (see page 103)?

If you are not happy with the training club, find another one. An inexperienced instructor who cannot handle a number of dogs in a confined environment can do more harm than good.

or carrying a stick or an umbrella.

- If you do not have children at home, make sure your Bulldog has a chance to meet and play with them. Bulldogs get on especially well with children, but your puppy needs to learn to be gentle and curb his more boisterous behaviour. Go to a local park and watch children in the play area. You will not be able to take your Bulldog inside the play area, but he will see children playing and will get used to their shouts of excitement.
- Attend puppy classes. These are designed for puppies between the ages of 12 to 20 weeks and give puppies a chance to play and interact together in a controlled,

supervised environment. As discussed earlier, this is extremely important for a Bulldog puppy. Your vet will have details of a local class.

- Take a walk around some quiet streets, such as a residential area, so your Bulldog can get used to the sound of traffic. As he becomes more confident, progress to busier areas. Remember, your lead is like a live wire and your feelings will travel directly to your Bulldog. Assume a calm, confident manner and your puppy will take the lead from you and have no reason to be fearful.
- Go to a railway station. You don't have to get on a train if you don't need to, but your Bulldog will have the chance to experience trains, people

wheeling luggage, loudspeaker announcements and going up and down stairs and over railway bridges.

- If you live in the town, plan a trip to the country. You can enjoy a day out and provide an opportunity for your Bulldog to see livestock, such as sheep, cattle and horses.
- One of the best places for socialising a dog is at a country fair. There will be crowds of people, livestock in pens, tractors, bouncy castles, fairground rides and food stalls.
- When your dog is over 20 weeks of age, locate a training class for adult dogs. You may find that your local training class has both puppy and adult classes.

An adolescent Bulldog may feel the need to question the status quo.

THE ADOLESCENT BULLDOG

It happens to every dog – and every owner. One minute you have an obedient well-behaved youngster and the next you have a boisterous adolescent who appears to have forgotten everything he ever learnt.

A Bulldog male will show adolescent behaviour from around 10 months. In terms of behavioural changes, a male often becomes more assertive as he pushes the boundaries to see if he can achieve top dog status.

This type of behaviour may continue until a dog reaches full maturity at around two years of age.

An adolescent female may become moody as she is coming into season – which is usually at around eight months – because of hormonal changes. She may prefer pleasing herself rather than trying to co-operate with you at this time. She may also become possessive over people, toys, or she may decide that she should take over the sofa. Again, a female may not settle in her

behaviour until she is fully mature at around two years old.

This can be a trying time, but it is important to retain a sense of perspective. Look at the situation from the dog's perspective and respond to uncharacteristic behaviour with firmness and consistency. Just like a teenager, an adolescent Bulldog feels the need to flex his muscles and challenge the status quo. But if you show that you are a strong leader (see page 80) and are quick to reward good behaviour, your Bulldog will be happy to accept you as his protector and provider.

WHEN THINGS GO WRONG

Positive, reward-based training has proved to be the most effective method of teaching dogs, but what happens when your Bulldog does something wrong and you need to show him that his behaviour is unacceptable? The old-fashioned school of dog training used to rely on the powers of punishment and negative reinforcement. A dog who raided the bin, for example, was smacked. Now we have learnt that it is not only unpleasant and cruel to hit a dog, it is also ineffective. If you hit a dog for stealing, he is more than likely to see you as the bad consequence of stealing, so he may raid the bin again, but probably not when you are around. If he raided the bin some time before you discovered it, he will be even more confused by your punishment, as he will not relate your response to his 'crime'.

A more commonplace example is when a dog fails to respond to a recall in the park. When the dog eventually comes back, the owner puts the dog on the lead and goes straight home to punish the dog for his poor response. Unfortunately, the dog will have a different interpretation. He does not think: "I won't ignore a recall command because the bad consequence is the end of my play in the park." He thinks: "Coming to my owner resulted in the end of playtime – therefore coming to my owner has a bad consequence, so I won't do that again."

There are a number of strategies to tackle undesirable behaviour – and they have nothing to do with harsh handling.

There are times when you need to call an instant halt to inappropriate behaviour.

Ignoring bad behaviour: The Bulldog is a strong-willed dog and a lot of undesirable behaviour in youngsters is to do with a lack of respect for his human family. For example, a young Bulldog that barks in a bid to get your attention is simply trying to assert his will. He believes he can demand your attention simply by making a noise. Even if you respond by shouting at him to tell him to "Be quiet" – he is still getting attention, so why inhibit his behaviour?

In this situation, the best and most effective response is to ignore your Bulldog. Do not speak to him and, even more importantly, do not look at him.

Withdraw your attention from him until he is quiet, and only then should you give him attention, but in a calm, controlled manner. Ideally, ask him to do something simple, such as a 'Sit', so you can reward him. It will not take long for him to realise that being quiet is the most effective strategy for getting what he wants. In this scenario, you have not only taught your Bulldog that he cannot demand your attention by barking, you have also earned his respect because you have taken control of the situation.

Stopping bad behaviour: There are occasions when you want to call an instant halt to whatever it is your Bulldog is doing. He may have just jumped on the sofa, or you may have caught him red-handed in the rubbish bin. He has already committed the 'crime', so your aim is to stop him and to redirect his attention. You can do this by using a deep, firm tone of voice to say "No", which will startle him, and then call him to you in a bright, happy voice. If necessary, you can attract him with a toy or a treat. The moment your Bulldog stops the undesirable behaviour and comes towards you, you can reward his good behaviour. You can back this up by running through a couple of simple exercises, such as a 'Sit' or a 'Down', and rewarding with

Despite your best efforts, you may find your Bulldog develops problematic behaviour.

treats. In this way, your Bulldog focuses his attention on you and sees you as the greatest source of reward and pleasure.

In a more extreme situation, when you want to interrupt undesirable behaviour and you know that a simple "No" will not do the trick, you can try something a little more dramatic. If you get a can and fill it with pebbles, or a plastic bottle and fill with dried pasta, it will make a really loud noise when you shake it or throw it. The same effect can be achieved with purpose-made training discs. The dog will be startled and stop what he is doing. Even better, the dog will not associate the unpleasant noise with you. This gives you the perfect opportunity to be the nice guy, calling the dog to you and giving him lots of praise.

PROBLEM BEHAVIOUR

If you have trained your Bulldog from puppyhood, survived his adolescence and established yourself as a fair and consistent leader, you will end up with a brilliant companion dog. The Bulldog is a well-balanced dog, who rarely has hang-ups if he has been correctly reared and socialised. Most Bulldogs are out-going, fun-loving and thrive on spending time with their owners. The most common cause of problem behaviour among Bulldogs is neglecting training in puppyhood so that a dog learns to follow his own agenda, and even tries to dominate his owners so that he can get his own way.

If you are worried about your Bulldog and feel out of your depth, do not delay in seeking professional help. This is readily available, usually through a referral from your vet, or you can find out additional information on the internet (see Appendices for web addresses). An animal behaviourist will have experience in tackling problem behaviour and will be able to help both you and your dog.

DOMINANCE/RESOURCE GUARDING

If you have trained and socialised your Bulldog correctly, he will know his place in the family pack and will have no desire to challenge your authority. As we have seen, adolescent males may test the boundaries, but this behaviour will not continue if you exhibit the necessary leadership skills.

However, if you have allowed your Bulldog to become over-assertive, he will express his dominance in a number of ways. This may include the following:

- Showing lack of respect for your personal space. For example, your dog will barge through doors ahead of you or jump up at you.
- Ignoring basic obedience commands.
- Showing no respect to younger members of the family, pushing amongst them and completely ignoring them.
- Male dogs may start marking (cocking their leg) in the house.
- Aggression towards people or other dogs (see page 102).
- A top-ranking Alpha female will pee in her own bedding, or in other dogs' beds to stake her claim. As soon as you put

98

clean bedding in the bed, she will put her scent on it!

However, the most common behaviour displayed by a Bulldog who has ideas above his station, is resource guarding. This may take a number of different forms:

- Getting up on to the sofa or your favourite armchair and refusing to move when you tell him to get back on the floor.
- Becoming possessive over a toy, or guarding his food bowl by lowering his head and staring when you get too close.
- Lowering his head and staring when anyone approaches his bed or when anyone gets too close to where he is lying.
- Dominance drinking – this is a throwback to 'guarding the water hole' from other animals or submissive members of the pack. A dominant dog will rush to the water bowl to drink – preventing other family animals from drinking – to display his dominance.

A Bulldog who is intent on guarding his food bowl needs to understand that you are in charge of his bowl.

In each of these scenarios, the Bulldog has something he values and he aims to keep it. He does not have sufficient respect for you, his human leader, to give up what he wants and he is 'warning' you to keep away.

If you see signs of your Bulldog behaving in this way, you must work at lowering his status so that he realises that you are the leader and he must accept your authority. Although you need to be firm, you also need to use positive training methods so that your Bulldog is rewarded for the behaviour you want. In this way, his 'correct' behaviour will be strengthened and repeated.

The golden rule is not to become confrontational. The dog will see this as a challenge and may become even more determined not to co-operate. There are a number of steps you can take to lower your Bulldog's status, which are far more likely to have a successful outcome. They include:

- Go back to basics and hold daily training sessions. Make sure you have some really tasty treats, or find a toy your Bulldog really values and only bring it out at training sessions. Run through all the training exercises you have taught your Bulldog. Remember, boredom is very often the key to undesirable behaviour. By giving him things to do, you are giving him mental stimulation and you have the opportunity to make a big fuss of him and reward him when he does well. This will help to reinforce the message that you are the leader and that it is rewarding to do as you ask.

RESOURCE GUARDING

He is allowed to eat when you give him permission.

If you drop in some extra food, your Bulldog will not see your interference as a threat.

- Teach your Bulldog something new; this can be as simple as learning a trick, such as shaking paws. Bulldogs excel at party tricks – begging, rollover, etc. Having something new to think about will mentally stimulate your Bulldog and he will benefit from interacting with you.
- Be 100 per cent consistent with all house rules – your Bulldog must never sit on the sofa and you must never allow him to jump up at you.
- If your Bulldog is becoming possessive over toys, remove all his toys and keep them out of reach. It is then up to you to decide when to produce a toy

and to initiate a game. Equally, it is you who will decide when the game is over and when to remove the toy. This teaches your Bulldog that you 'own' his toys. He has fun playing and interacting with you, but the game is over – and the toy is given up – when you say so. The best method of getting your Bulldog to give up a toy is to play swaps – offering a treat in exchange for the toy. It does not take the Bulldog long to realise that it is worth his while to give up his toy in return for a tasty treat.

- If your Bulldog has been guarding his food bowl, put the bowl down empty and

drop in a little food at a time. Periodically stop dropping in the food and tell your Bulldog "Sit" and "Wait". Give it a few seconds and then reward him by dropping in more food. This shows your Bulldog that you are the provider of the food and he can only eat when you allow him to.

- Make sure the family eats before you feed your Bulldog. Some trainers advocate eating in front of the dog (maybe just a few bites from a biscuit) before starting a training session, so the dog appreciates your elevated status.
- Do not let your Bulldog barge through doors ahead of you or

leap from the back of the car before you release him. You may need to put your dog on the lead and teach him to "Wait" at doorways and then reward him for letting you go through first.

If your Bulldog is progressing well with his retraining programme, think about getting involved with a dog sport, such as agility or obedience. This will give your Bulldog a positive outlet for his energies. However, if your Bulldog is still seeking to be dominant, or you have any other concerns, do not delay in seeking the help of an animal behaviourist, although you should first check that they have experience with Bulldogs. You could also join a local Bulldog club and seek help and advice from experienced Bulldog owners.

Give your Bulldog a boredom busting toy to keep him occupied when you go out.

SEPARATION ANXIETY

A Bulldog should be brought up to accept short periods of separation from his owner so that he does not become anxious. A new puppy should be left for short periods on his own, ideally in a crate where he cannot get up to any mischief. It is a good idea to leave him with a boredom-busting toy so he will be happily occupied in your absence. When you return, do not rush to the crate and make a huge fuss. Wait a few minutes, and then calmly go to the crate and release your dog, telling him how good he has been. If this scenario is repeated a number of times, your Bulldog

will soon learn that being left on his own is no big deal.

Problems with separation anxiety are most likely to arise if you take on a rescued dog who has major insecurities. You may also find your Bulldog hates being left if you have failed to accustom him to short periods of isolation when he was growing up. Separation anxiety is expressed in a number of ways and all are equally distressing for both dog and owner. An anxious dog who is left alone may bark and whine continuously, urinate and defecate, and may be extremely destructive.

There are a number of steps you can take when attempting to solve this problem.

- Put up a baby-gate between adjoining rooms and leave your dog in one room while you are in the other room. Your dog will be able to see you and hear you, but he is learning to cope without being right next to you. Build up the amount of time you can leave your dog in easy stages.

- Buy some boredom-busting toys and fill them with some tasty treats. Whenever you leave your dog, give him a food-filled toy so that he is busy while you are away.

- If you have not used a crate before, it is not too late to start. Make sure the crate is cosy and train your Bulldog to get used to going in his crate while you are in the same room. Gradually build up the amount of time he spends in the crate and then start leaving the room for short periods. When you return, do not make a fuss of your dog. Leave him for five or ten minutes before releasing him, so that he gets used to your comings and goings.

- Pretend to go out, putting on your coat and jangling keys, but do not leave the house. An anxious dog often becomes hyped up by the ritual of leaving and this will help to desensitize him.

- When you go out, leave a radio or a TV on. Some dogs are

CONTROLLED INTERACTION

Give your Bulldog the opportunity to meet dogs of sound temperament in a controlled situation.

The younger Bulldog (left) approaches the adult.

The adult's body language is unchanged so the youngster has no need to feel apprehensive.

A calm, controlled meeting where neither dog feels threatened.

comforted by hearing voices and background noise when they are left alone.
• Try to make your absences as short as possible when you are first training your dog to accept being on his own.

If you take these steps, your dog should become less anxious, and, over a period of time, you should be able to solve the problem. However, if you are failing to make progress, do not delay in calling in expert help.

AGGRESSION
Aggression is a complex issue, as there are different causes and the behaviour may be triggered by numerous factors. It may be directed towards people, but far more commonly it is directed towards other dogs. Aggression in dogs may be the result of:
• **Dominance:** See page 98.
• **Defensive behaviour:** This may be induced by fear, pain or punishment.
• **Territory:** A dog may become aggressive if strange dogs or people enter his territory (which is generally seen as the house and garden).
• **Intra-sexual issues:** This is aggression between sexes – male-to-male or female-to-female.
• **Parental instinct:** A mother dog may become aggressive if she is protecting her puppies.

  The Bulldog was originally bred to be a fighting dog, and he may take to the offensive if he feels threatened or if he is provoked.

But there is no doubt that a dog who has been well socialised – with sufficient exposure to other dogs at significant stages of his development – will stand a far better chance of interacting peacefully.

However, you may have taken on an older, rescued dog that has been poorly socialised and there is something in his history that has made him aggressive. Or you may have a dog who has become dominant in his own home and family and so he is assertive in his dealings with other dogs, as he believes he is top dog.

If dominance is the underlying cause, you can try the measures outlined in this chapter. Equally if your dog has been poorly socialised, you can try to make up for lost time and work with other dogs of sound temperament in controlled situations. But if you are concerned about your dog's behaviour, you would be well advised to call in professional help. If the aggression is directed towards people, you should seek immediate advice. This behaviour can escalate very quickly and could lead to disastrous consequences.

If your Bulldog is enjoying his training why not try some more advanced work.

NEW CHALLENGES

If you enjoy training your Bulldog, you may want to try one of the many dog sports that are now on offer. In the UK, owners tend to limit activities if their dog is not a natural working breed, such as a Border Collie or a German Shepherd Dog. However, in the United States, owners are much more prepared to 'have a go', and Bulldogs have made their mark in a number of sports.

GOOD CITIZEN SCHEME

This is a scheme run by the Kennel Club in the UK and the American Kennel Club in the USA. The schemes promote responsible ownership and help

you to train a well-behaved dog who will fit in with the community. The schemes are excellent for all pet owners and they are also a good starting point if you plan to compete with your Bulldog when he is older. The KC and the AKC schemes vary in format. In the UK there are three levels: bronze, silver and gold, with each test becoming progressively more demanding. In the AKC scheme there is a single test.

Some of the exercises include:

- Walking on a loose lead among people and other dogs.
- Recall amid distractions.
- A controlled greeting where dogs stay under control while their owners meet.
- The dog allows all-over grooming and handling by his owner, and also accepts being handled by the examiner.
- Stays, with the owner in sight and then out of sight.
- Food manners, allowing the owner to eat without begging and taking a treat on command.
- Sendaway – sending the dog to his bed.

The tests are designed to show the control you have over your dog and his ability to respond correctly and remain calm in all situations. The Good Citizen Scheme is taught at most training clubs. For more information, log on to the Kennel Club or AKC website (see Appendices).

SHOWING

In your eyes, your Bulldog is the most perfect dog in the world – but would a judge agree? Showing is a highly competitive sport, but many owners get bitten by the showing bug, and their calendar is governed by the dates of the top showing fixtures.

To be successful in the show ring, a Bulldog must conform as closely as possible to the Breed Standard, which is a written blueprint describing the 'perfect' Bulldog (see Chapter Seven). To get started you need to buy a puppy that has show potential and then train him to perform in the ring. A Bulldog will be expected to stand in show pose, gait for the judge in order to show off his natural movement, and to be examined by the judge. This involves a detailed hands-on examination, so your Bulldog must be bombproof when handled by strangers.

Many training clubs hold ringcraft classes, which are run by

Showing is highly competitive at the top level. This is Kanchee Kast No Shadow In Kofyn.

experienced showgoers. At these classes, you will learn how to handle your Bulldog in the ring, and you will also find out about rules, procedures and show-ring etiquette.

The best plan is to start off at some small, informal shows where you can practise and learn the tricks of the trade before graduating to bigger shows. It's a long haul starting in the very first puppy class, but the dream is to make your Bulldog up into a Champion. Joining your local Bulldog club is a great way of learning all about showing.

COMPETITIVE OBEDIENCE

Border Collies and German Shepherds dominate this sport, but there is no reason why you and your Bulldog should not see if you can master the exercises. The classes start off being relatively easy and become progressively more challenging with additional exercises, and the handler giving minimal instructions to the dog.

Exercises include:

• **Heelwork**: Dog and handler must complete a set pattern on and off the lead, which includes left turns, right turns, about turns and changes of pace.
• **Recall**: This may be when the handler is stationary or on the move.
• **Retrieve**: This may be a dumbbell or any article chosen by the judge.
• **Sendaway**: The dog is sent to a designated spot and must go into an instant 'Down' until he is recalled by the handler.
• **Stays**: The dog must stay in the 'Sit' and in the 'Down' for a set amount of time. In advanced classes, the handler is out of sight.
• **Scent**: The dog must retrieve a single cloth from a pre-arranged pattern of cloths that has his owner's scent, or, in advanced classes, the judge's scent. There may also be decoy cloths.
• **Distance control**: The dog

must execute a series of moves ('Sit', 'Stand', 'Down') without moving from his position and with the handler at a distance.

Even though competitive obedience requires accuracy and precision, make it fun for your Bulldog, with lots of praise and rewards so that you motivate him to do his best. Many training clubs run advanced classes for those who want to compete in obedience, or you can hire the services of a professional trainer for one-on-one sessions.

AGILITY

This fun sport has grown enormously in popularity over the past few years, and if you keep your Bulldog fit and lean, there is no reason why he should not enjoy the sport.

In agility competitions, each dog must complete a set course over a series of obstacles, which include:

- Jumps (upright hurdles and long jump, varying in height – small, medium and large, depending on the size of the dog)
- Weaves
- A-frame
- Dog walk
- Seesaw
- Tunnels (collapsible and rigid)
- Tyre

Dogs may compete in Jumping classes, with jumps, tunnels and weaves, or in Agility classes, which have the full set of equipment. Faults are awarded for poles down on the jumps, missed contact points on the A-frame, dog walk and seesaw, and refusals. If a dog takes the wrong course, he is eliminated. The winner is the dog that completes the course in the fastest time with no faults. As you progress up the levels, courses become progressively

harder with more twists, turns and changes of direction.

If you want to get involved in Agility, you will need to find a club that specialises in the sport (see Appendices). You will not be allowed to start training until your Bulldog is 12 months old and you cannot compete until he is 18 months old. This rule is for the protection of the dog, who may suffer injury if he puts strain on bones and joints while he is still growing.

SUMMING UP

The Bulldog is an outstanding companion dog – and once you have owned one, no other breed will do. He is intelligent, fun-loving, affectionate and loyal. Make sure you keep your half of the bargain: spend time socialising and training your Bulldog so that you can be proud to take him anywhere and he will always be a credit to you.

There is no reason why a fit Bulldog should not enjoy the challenge of agility.

THE PERFECT BULLDOG

Chapter 7

I have judged Bulldogs all around the world as well as numerous times in the UK at Championship show level, and, to date, I have not found the perfect specimen. I have, however, been lucky enough to have seen and to have judged a number who came close to it. Perfection is something that all serious Bulldog breeders strive to achieve every time they breed a new litter. We watch the new pups grow with anticipation, always hoping that among them will be a Champion in the making.

In attempting to breed the perfect Bulldog, the first thing is to be aware of the Breed Standard. All pedigree dogs have their own Standard, which has, generally, been written by early aficionados of the breed. Most, with a few minor alterations, remain the same to this day. As the Bulldog is a British native breed, our Kennel Club Standard is adopted by the Federation Cynologique Internationale (FCI), which is the governing body for most countries outside of the United Kingdom and North America. The American Kennel Club Standard is slightly different to ours. These differences will be highlighted later.

The purpose of all Breed Standards is to describe to the reader the physical conformation, character and temperament of the breed in question. If interpreted correctly, it describes the ideal specimen of the breed – something that all serious breeders strive to achieve, and used by judges as the template when deciding on placements in the show ring.

HOW THE BREED STANDARD DEVELOPED

The first Bulldog Standard was written and published by the Bulldog Club Incorporated on 27 May 1875. This Standard remained the same until a change in the desired weight, increasing it by 5 lbs (2.3 kgs) for both sexes in the early 1950s.

In 1986, along with many other breeds, the Kennel Club in its wisdom decided to revise the Standard. The main reason for this, in the Bulldog's case, was to explain the Standard in plainer English, especially the finer points. After long discussions and deliberations, the Bulldog Breed Council, with the backing of the Kennel Club, made some more changes in 2003. These were done mainly with the health and well-being of the breed in mind. Changes were made to some of the more exaggerated terms, making sure that judges would penalise these, together with any degree of unsoundness.

In 2009, the Kennel Club again

altered the Bulldog Standard, asking for no input from the Breed Council, which proved to be very divisive. The Bulldog Standard, as far as I am aware, is the most complex of any breed, with a great deal of it being taken up by the head properties. This is why the breed is sometimes referred to in dog showing circles as 'a head breed', and why some judges only appear to judge the dog's head and front, and not worry about what is going on behind the shoulders. This is, of course, wrong and some of the changes to the Standard in 2003 and 2009 were brought in to try to rectify this.

FIT FOR FUNCTION

As our breed is pretty well man-made, the Bulldog is put together like no other. The judge must therefore put aside all thoughts of how other, more natural dogs are put together or move. However, the Bulldog, like all breeds, was bred to perform a specific task – in his case, the so-called 'sport' of bull baiting, and, if put together properly, a modern day Bulldog should still be "fit for function".

The Bulldog's most unique physical characteristic is probably his undershot jaw, which held a lockjaw on the bull's flesh. His laidback nose helped the dog to breathe while retaining his grip, and the forehead and face wrinkles directed the bull's blood away from the dog's eyes. The Bulldog's low-to-ground front helped him stave off the bull's

frontal attacks, while the shortness of his hocks provided excellent stamina and power in the backend. The loose skin of the dog helped to prevent the bull's horns penetrating vital organs. The physical structure of the Bulldog allowed him to perform his barbaric task with remarkable efficiency.

ANALYSIS AND INTEPRETATION

For the purposes of this book I have reproduced the UK's Kennel Club Breed Standard and the American Kennel Club Breed Standard, followed by my analysis of the two. As mentioned earlier, the Federation Cynologique Internationale (FCI) adopts the UK Standard, as the Bulldog is a native British breed.

The Bulldog is a man-made breed, and should be judged accordingly.

KC

GENERAL APPEARANCE
Smooth-coated, fairly thick set, rather low in stature, broad, powerful and compact. Head fairly large in proportion to size but no point so much in excess of others as to destroy the general symmetry, or make the dog appear deformed, or interfere with its powers of motion. Face relatively short, muzzle broad, blunt and inclined upwards although not excessively so. Dogs showing respiratory distress highly undesirable. Body fairly short, well knit, limbs stout, well muscled and in hard condition with no tendency towards obesity. Hindquarters high and strong. Bitches not so grand or well developed as dogs.

AKC

GENERAL APPEARANCE
The perfect Bulldog must be of medium size and smooth coat; with heavy, thick-set, low-swung body, massive short-faced head, wide shoulders and sturdy limbs. The general appearance and attitude should suggest great stability, vigor and strength. The disposition should be equable and kind, resolute and courageous (not vicious or aggressive), and demeanor should be pacific and dignified. These attributes should be countenanced by the expression and behavior.

This heading has two significant

Top winning UK dog
Ch. Kelloe White Glove
– Breed Record Holder
with 50 CCs.

A trio of top-winning
American Bulldogs: Ch.
Adamant Warlock, Ch.
Silverspoon's Nothing
Personal and Ch.
Silverspoon's Just
Peachy.

Top winning FCI dog:
Int. Ch. Jabberwocky's
Cloudless, a prolific
winner under FCI rules.

differences between the Standards, both of which were changes to the UK Standard that were made in 2003 with the health of the dog being uppermost in mind. These are the respiratory clause, and also the word 'massive', which was removed from the UK Standard to try to get rid of the grossly overdone animals seen in years gone by.

KC

CHARACTERISTICS AND TEMPERAMENT

Conveys impression of determination, strength and activity. Alert, bold, loyal, dependable, courageous, fierce in appearance, but possessed of affectionate nature

AKC

TEMPERAMENT

The disposition should be equable and kind, resolute and courageous (not vicious or aggressive), and demeanor should be pacific and dignified. These attributes should be countenanced by the expression and behavior.

Although worded differently, both of these descriptions sum up the Bulldog's character and temperament perfectly.

KC

HEAD AND SKULL,

Skull relatively large in circumference. Viewed from front appears high from corner of lower jaw to apex of skull; also broad and square. Cheeks well rounded and extended sideways beyond eyes. Viewed from side, head appears very high and moderately short from back to point of nose. Forehead flat with skin on and about head slightly loose and finely wrinkled without excess, neither prominent nor overhanging face.

From defined stop, a furrow extending to middle of skull being traceable to apex. Face from front of cheek bone to nose, relatively short, skin may be slightly wrinkled. Muzzle short, broad, turned upwards and deep from corner of eye to corner of mouth. Nose and nostrils large, broad and black, under no circumstances liver colour, red or brown.

Distance from inner corner of eye (or from centre of stop between eyes) to extreme tip of nose should not be less than distance from tip of the nose to edge of the underlip. Nostrils large wide and open, with well defined vertical straight line between. Flews (chops) thick, broad and deep, covering lower jaws at sides, but joining underlip in front. Teeth not visible. Jaws broad, strong and square, lower jaw slightly projecting in front of upper with moderate turn up. Over

Enormous importance is placed on the correct proportions and appearance of the head.

nose wrinkle, if present, whole or broken, must never adversely affect or obscure eyes or nose. Pinched nostrils and heavy over nose roll are unacceptable and should be heavily penalised. Viewed from front, the various properties of the face must be equally balanced on either side of an imaginary line down centre.

EYES

Seen from front, situated low down in skull, well away from ears. Eyes and stop in same straight line, at right angles to furrow. Wide apart, but outer corners within the outline of cheeks. Round, of moderate size, neither sunken nor prominent, in colour very dark – almost black – showing no white when looking directly forward. Free from obvious eye problems.

The 'rose' ear, which should be small and thin, is correct for the breed.

EARS

Set high – i.e. front edge of each ear (as viewed from front) joins outline of skull at top corner of such outline, so as to place them as wide apart, as high and as far from eyes as possible. Small and thin. 'Rose ear' correct, i.e. folding inwards back, upper or front inner edge curving outwards and backwards, showing part of inside of burr.

MOUTH

Jaws broad and square with six small front teeth between canines in an even row. Canines wide apart. Teeth large and strong, not seen when mouth closed. When viewed from front under jaw directly under upper jaw and parallel.

AKC

HEAD

EYES AND EYELIDS

The eyes, seen from the front, should be situated low down the skull, as far from the ears as possible, and their corners should be in a straight line at right angles with the stop. They should be quite in front of the head, as wide apart as possible, provided their outer corners are within the outline of the cheeks when viewed from the front. They should be quite round in form, of moderate size, neither sunken nor bulging, and in color should be very dark. The lids should cover the white of the eyeball, when the dog is looking directly forward, and the lid should show no "haw".

EARS

The ears should be set high in the head, the front inner edge of each ear joining the outline of the skull at the top back corner of skull, so as to place

NOSE

A full nose roll – this should not be so full as to affect the nostrils, and therefore the dog's ability to breath.

A split nose roll – the most desirable nose roll. The original nose roll was a split one.

This nose roll would be considered too full, according to the new British Standard.

them as wide apart, and as high, and as far from the eyes as possible. In size they should be small and thin. The shape termed "rose ear" is the most desirable. The rose ear folds inward at its back lower edge, the upper front edge curving over, outward and backward, showing part of the inside of the burr. (The ears should not be carried erect or prick-eared or buttoned and should never be cropped.)

SKULL
The skull should be very large, and in circumference, in front of the ears, should measure at least the height of the dog at the shoulders. Viewed from the front, it should appear very high from the corner of the lower jaw to the apex of the skull, and

also very broad and square. Viewed at the side, the head should appear very high, and very short from the point of the nose to occiput. The forehead should be flat (not rounded or domed), neither too prominent nor overhanging the face.

CHEEKS
The cheeks should be well rounded, protruding sideways and outward beyond the eyes.

STOP
The temples or frontal bones should be very well defined, broad, square and high, causing a hollow or groove between the eyes. This indentation, or stop, should be both broad and deep and extend up the middle of the forehead, dividing the head

vertically, being traceable to the top of the skull.

FACE AND MUZZLE
The face, measured from the front of the cheekbone to the tip of the nose, should be extremely short, the muzzle being very short, broad, turned upward and very deep from the corner of the eye to the corner of the mouth.

NOSE
The nose should be large, broad and black, its tip set back deeply between the eyes. The distance from bottom of stop, between the eyes, to the tip of nose should be as short as possible and not exceed the length from the tip of nose to the edge of under lip. The nostrils should be wide, large

112

JAWS AND BITE

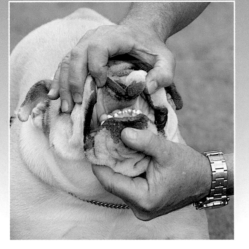

The correct bite is undershot, with the lower jaw projecting in front of the upper jaw.

and black, with a well-defined line between them. Any nose other than black is objectionable and a brown or liver-colored nose shall disqualify.

LIPS

The chops or "flews" should be thick, broad, pendant and very deep, completely overhanging the lower jaw at each side. They join the under lip in front and almost or quite cover the teeth, which should be scarcely noticeable when the mouth is closed.

BITE/JAWS

The jaws should be massive, very broad, square and "undershot," the lower jaw projecting considerably in front of the upper jaw and turning up. The teeth should be large and strong, with the canine teeth or tusks wide apart, and the six small teeth in front, between the canines, in an even, level row.

The head of the Bulldog is, without doubt, the most important and distinguishing feature of the breed. The old Standard's points system allotted a total of 45 out of 100 to it, with the present-day American Standard still allotting 39 points. With such complicated head points to consider when judging, you would think it would be a very difficult task. However, once you understand the points fully, this could not be further from the truth. Because of its complexity, if just a couple of faults are present, the whole balance of the dog's head is obviously wrong.

As far as the two Standards are concerned, since the new UK Standard of October 2009 there are quite a few major differences. Only time will tell whether or not the AKC will follow suit and change their Standard accordingly. One of the main differences is with regard to the nose roll (if present). As a breed, we were getting some large rolls that, in extreme cases, were hindering the dog's nostrils, thereby affecting his breathing. To this end the clause: "Nose roll must not interfere with the line of the layback" was adopted in 2003 and changed again in 2009 to: "must never adversely affect or obscure eyes or nose. Pinched nostrils and heavy over nose roll are unacceptable and should be heavily penalized".

Ideally, you should be able to lay a straight edge from the point of the jaw to the forehead without the nose roll interfering. The American Standard, when dealing with skin, calls for a heavily wrinkled head. The UK version, in my opinion, is the better as a fine, wrinkled head, health-wise, is much to be preferred although not so finely wrinkled as to produce a plain head.

The Bulldog's mouth should be very broad and square with the lower jaw in the front of the upper and sweeping up. The teeth should be large and strong with the canines set wide apart and level. A wry jaw, i.e. one where the lower canines are not completely straight and level, is most undesirable. An unfortunate fault, which is creeping into the breed, is that of a very narrow underjaw. This, coupled with wryness, is a very serious fault, as a narrow jaw usually lacks upsweep and is always lacking in strength.

The ears are, in my opinion, the one head feature, which, if not the correct 'rose ear', spoil the whole expression of the dog. Probably the most common of ear faults to be seen in the ring today are the button and tulip ears, which, again, are highly undesirable.

The nose of the Bulldog is like no other breed, it should be large and broad and laid back deeply between the eyes. The nostrils should be large and open, with a well-defined line between them. They should not be pinched in any way. In the American points scale of judging, the nose carries the largest number of all other breed points.

With the head taking up so much of our Standard, it is understandable that so much time and consideration should be given to it when judging.

KC

NECK AND BODY
Moderate in length, thick, deep and strong. Well arched at back, with some loose, thick and wrinkled skin about throat, forming slight dewlap on each side. Chest wide, prominent and deep. Back short, strong, broad at shoulders. Slight fall to back close behind shoulders (lowest part) whence spine should rise to loins (top higher than top of shoulder), curving again more suddenly to tail, forming slight arch – a distinctive characteristic of breed. Body well ribbed up behind with belly tucked up and not pendulous.

AKC

NECK
The neck should be short, very thick, deep and strong and well arched at the back.

TOPLINE
There should be a slight fall in the back, close behind the shoulders (its lowest part), whence the spine should rise to the loins (the top of which should be higher than the top of the shoulders), thence curving again more suddenly to the tail, forming an arch (a very distinctive feature of the breed),

The curved topline is a unique feature of the breed.

termed "roach back" or, more correctly, "wheel-back."

BODY

The brisket and body should be very capacious, with full sides, well-rounded ribs and very deep from the shoulders down to its lowest part, where it joins the chest. It should be well let down between the shoulders and forelegs, giving the dog a broad, low, short-legged appearance.

CHEST

The chest should be very broad, deep and full.

UNDERLINE

The body should be well ribbed up behind with the belly tucked up and not rotund.

BACK AND LOIN

The back should be short and strong, very broad at the shoulders and comparatively narrow at the loins.

The Bulldog's topline is virtually unique to our breed, and is a finer point that is often overlooked or misunderstood by new judges. The correct roach back should rise over the loins with the top of the roach slightly higher than the top of the shoulder. The topline should then drop sharply down to a relatively low-set tail.

The term 'roach back' was removed from the Standard in the 2009 change, much to

the consternation of the breed, as the KC left this terminology in the Standard of the French Bulldog.

There are three faulty toplines, all of which, to a greater or lesser degree, can be seen in the ring today. The camel back is where the rise is over the rib rather than the loin; the sway back is caused by too great a fall away behind the shoulder, giving a 'ski slope' effect; the straight back speaks for itself.

It is only with the correct roach that you also get the right tuck-up underneath. The sway-backed dog also often has a gay or high-set tail, although I have also seen these on dogs with good toplines.

The shoulders are broad and very powerful; the front legs are stout, thick and muscular.

One of the things that annoys me – and, I am sure, many others in the show ring – is when a judge asks a class of Bulldogs to turn side on so that he can see all the toplines together. Then, lo and behold, he awards the class to a dog with a very bad topline!

KC

FOREQUARTERS

Shoulders broad, sloping and deep, very powerful and muscular giving appearance of being 'tacked on' body. Brisket round and deep. Well let down between forelegs. Ribs not flat-sided, but well rounded. Forelegs very stout and strong, well developed, set wide apart, thick, muscular and straight, bones of legs large and straight, not bandy nor curved and short in proportion to hindlegs, but not so short as to make back appear long, or detract from dog's activity. Elbows low and standing well away from ribs. Pasterns short, straight and strong.

AKC

SHOULDERS

The shoulders should be muscular, very heavy, widespread and slanting outward, giving stability and great power.

FORELEGS

The forelegs should be short, very stout, straight and muscular, set wide apart, with well developed calves, presenting a bowed outline, but the bones of the legs should not be curved or bandy, nor the feet brought too close together.

ELBOWS
The elbows should be low and stand well out and loose from the body.

FEET
The feet should be moderate in size, compact and firmly set. Toes compact, well split up, with high knuckles and very short stubby nails. The front feet may be straight or slightly out-turned.

You can see from both these descriptions that the Standard calls for well-boned, straight legs not in any way bowed or 'Queen Anne', a feature that many laymen foolishly think the Bulldog should have.

KC

HINDQUARTERS
Legs large and muscular, slightly longer in proportion than forelegs. Hocks slightly bent, well let down; legs long and muscular from loins to hock. Stifles turned very slightly outwards away from body.

FEET
Fore, straight and turning very slightly outward; of medium size and moderately round. Hind, round and compact. Toes compact and thick, well split

up, making knuckles prominent and high.

AKC

LEGS
The hind legs should be strong and muscular and longer than the forelegs, so as to elevate the loins above the shoulders. Hocks should be slightly bent and well let down, so as to give length and strength from the loins to hock. The lower leg should be short, straight and strong, with the stifles turned slightly outward and away from the body. The hocks are thereby made to approach each other, and the hind feet to turn outward.

The hindlegs, which are strong and muscular, should be longer than the front legs.

FEET
The feet should be moderate in size, compact and firmly set. Toes compact, well split up, with high knuckles and short stubby nails. The hind feet should be pointed well outward.

There is an old saying in the horse world – "no foot no horse" – and the same can be applied to dogs. A bad foot usually means that there are problems in the overall construction of the dog. The feet should be moderate in size, compact, and firmly set with toes well slit up with high knuckles. Splayed feet and hare feet with week pasterns are the main faults seen when judging. These dogs generally do not move as a Bulldog should.

KC

TAIL
Set on low, jutting out rather straight and then turning downwards. Round, smooth and devoid of fringe or coarse hair. Moderate in length – rather short than long – thick at root, tapering quickly to a fine point. Downward carriage (not having a decided upward curve at end) and never carried above back.

AKC

TAIL
The tail may be either straight or "screwed" (but never curved or curly), and in any case must be short, hung low, with

TAIL SETS

Good tail set.

Correct pump-handled tail.

Well-set tail – a little short but free-moving.

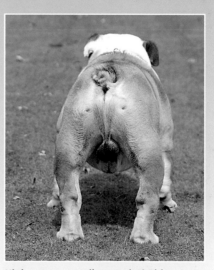

High-set screw tail – not desirable.

GAIT AND MOVEMENT

The wide-set front legs move straight forward from the shoulder.

The hind legs should hit the ground closer together than the front legs.

decided downward carriage, thick root and fine tip. If straight, the tail should be cylindrical and of uniform taper. If "screwed", the bends or kinks should be well defined, and they may be abrupt and even knotty, but no portion of the member should be elevated above the base or root.

Here you will see that the KC Standard calls for an exclusively straight tail whereas the US version allows a screw tail. In reality, the screw tail is also very prevalent in the UK and rarely penalised in the show ring. When the Standard was being changed in 2009, the Bulldog Breed Council asked for a clause penalising a badly screwed tail on health grounds, but this was turned down,

Happily, in recent years, the straight tail is increasingly becoming the norm. This has been done in the main with selective breeding. The Bulldog tail is never docked and each pup in a litter will have a different tail in both shape, size and type.

KC

GAIT/MOVEMENT
Appearing to walk with short, quick steps on tips of toes, hind feet not lifted high, appearing to skim ground, running with one or other shoulder rather advanced. Soundness of movement of the utmost importance.

AKC

GAIT
The style and carriage are peculiar, his gait being a loose-

The texture of the coat is fine and close, and the colour should be pure and brilliant.

jointed, shuffling, sidewise motion, giving the characteristic "roll". The action must, however, be unrestrained, free and vigorous.

Bulldog movement is something unique to our breed. If a Bulldog is put together correctly, he should move with a rather restrained gait but never unsoundly. His wide-set front legs, narrow loin and longer rear legs give him a peculiar, rolling movement – the forelegs going straight forward from his wide "tacked on" shoulder. Weak shoulders or a narrow front result in the dog's front legs 'plaiting', with the legs going under the dog when viewed from the front. The rear legs should hit the ground closer together than the front legs. The rolling movement is the result of the overall conformation of the dog, and faults in the body will nearly always result in poor movement.

KC

COAT AND COLOUR
Fine texture, short, close and smooth (hard only from shortness and closeness, not wiry).

COLOUR
Whole or smut, (i.e. whole colour with black mask or muzzle). Only whole colours (which should be brilliant and pure of their sort) viz., brindles, reds with their various shades, fawns, fallows etc., white and pied (i.e. combination of white with any of the foregoing colours). Dudley, black and black with tan highly undesirable.

In terms of show presentation, the Bulldog is a low-maintenance breed.

AKC

COAT
The coat should be straight, short, flat, close, of fine texture, smooth and glossy. (No fringe, feather or curl.)

SKIN
The skin should be soft and loose, especially at the head, neck and shoulders.

WRINKLES AND DEWLAP
The head and face should be covered with heavy wrinkles, and at the throat, from jaw to chest, there should be two loose pendulous folds, forming the dewlap.

COLOUR OF COAT
The colour of coat should be uniform, pure of its kind and brilliant. The various colors found in the breed are to be preferred in the following order: (1) red brindle, (2) all other brindles, (3) solid white, (4) solid red, fawn or fallow, (5) piebald, (6) inferior qualities of all the foregoing. Note: A perfect piebald is preferable to a muddy brindle or defective solid color. Solid black is very undesirable, but not so objectionable if occurring to a moderate degree in piebald patches. The brindles to be perfect should have a fine, even and equal distribution of the composite colors. In

brindles and solid colors a small white patch on the chest is not considered detrimental. In piebalds the color patches should be well defined, of pure color and symmetrically distributed.

The US Standard has a color preference for judges, which, in reality, is almost impossible to achieve when judging a large class. The UK Standard states that the colour black is highly undesirable whereas the US allows solid black as long as it is in piebald patches. Colour is one of the things that, in Bulldogs at least, is very difficult to breed for. Generally, brindle can be quite dominant, but we

Bulldogs that are lighter in frame are now being favoured in the UK.

recently bred a litter of just one pup whose mother was brindle-and-white and whose father was red brindle-and-white. He turned out to be a gorgeous bright red-and-white. Whites and fawns are probably the most likely to reproduce themselves if bred together. Having said this, the largest litter we have bred was one of nine, with a red-and-white bitch mated to a white dog and we got a real mixture of colours and markings. You never can tell.

KC

SIZE
Dogs: 25 kgs (55 lbs); bitches: 23 kgs (50 lbs).

AKC

SIZE
The size for mature dogs is about 50 pounds; for mature bitches about 40 pounds.

PROPORTION
The circumference of the skull in front of the ears should measure at least the height of the dog at the shoulders.

SYMMETRY
The "points" should be well distributed and bear good relation one to the other, no feature being in such prominence from either excess or lack of quality that the animal appears deformed or ill-proportioned.

INFLUENCE OF SEX
In comparison of specimens of different sex, due allowance should be made in favor of the bitches, which do not bear the characteristics of the breed to the same degree of perfection and grandeur as do the dogs.

The size difference in the two Standards bears no reality in the show ring. Having judged the breed in America on a number of occasions, I can say that the top-winning dogs are at least 10-15 lbs (4.5 – 6.8 kgs) over their Standard. Until recently the same could be said about dogs in the UK, but in recent times the big, heavy, overdone dogs that could win a few years ago are no longer being put up by judges, who have the health and welfare of the breed at heart.

KC

FAULTS

Any departure from the foregoing points should be considered a fault and the seriousness with which the fault should be regarded should be in exact proportion to its degree and its effect upon the health and welfare of the dog.

Note: Male animals should have two apparently normal testicles fully descended into the scrotum.

AKC

DISQUALIFICATION
Brown or liver-colored nose.

The US Standard does not actually ask for two normally descended testicles. Indeed, it doesn't ask for any at all! However, it is not a disqualification in the UK Standard although the dog would have to be an outstanding example to be considered for top honours in the show ring if he is monorchid. A cryptorchid dog, i.e. with none at all, would never be considered.

AMERICAN SCALE OF POINTS		
General Properties		
Proportion and symmetry	5	
Attitude	3	
Expression	2	
Gait	3	
Size	3	
Coat	2	
Color of coat	4	
Sub Total		22
Head		
Skull	5	
Cheeks	2	
Stop	4	
Eyes and eyelids	3	
Ears	5	
Wrinkle	5	
Nose	6	
Chops	2	
Jaws	5	
Teeth	2	
Sub Total		39
Body, Legs, etc.		
Neck	3	
Dewlap	2	
Shoulders	5	
Chest	3	
Ribs	3	
Brisket	2	
Belly	2	
Back	5	
Forelegs and elbows	4	
Hind Legs	3	
Feet	3	
Tail	4	
Sub Total		39
TOTAL		100

SUMMING UP
When judging the Bulldog, it should always be remembered that if any dog is to come close to the Breed Standard, he must, first and foremost, have 'type' and be balanced all through –

and, certainly in the current anti-dog climate, he must be sound, healthy, free of any undue exaggerations, and have an excellent temperament.

Although the Standard is complex, if the judge has a

It is important to look at the dog as a whole – including his temperament – which is perhaps the most important consideration of all.

picture of how the 'perfect' Bulldog should look and move, he should hopefully transfer it to his placings in the show ring. Again, because of its complexity, fault judging can be, for some, the easiest way to sort out a class of dogs. Although easy, this type of judging is, in my opinion, nearly as bad as the 'friends and family' approach.

Faults should always be treated in a kind way, as there has not yet been a dog born with no faults at all. For me, the most serious faults, which I consider should be heavily penalised, are lack of type, unsoundness of any sort and – probably the worst of all for a Bulldog – bad temperament.

I hope that this analysis has helped both the novice judge and the more experienced to understand the blueprint of the breed that the Standard represents. It is in the hands of these new and upcoming breeders and judges to see that this wonderful breed is preserved for the enjoyment of future generations. As far as the new Standard, which came into force in October 2009, is concerned, only time will tell if the AKC and FCI adopt it as the Standard from the 'country of origin'. Somehow I doubt that they will!

HAPPY AND HEALTHY

The Bulldog is a stoical dog with a life-span that may reach double figures, provided his needs are met. The Bulldog is renowned as a plucky, faithful companion and a willing friend on a non-conditional basis. He will, however, of necessity rely on you for food and shelter, accident prevention and medication. A healthy Bulldog is a happy chap, looking to please and amuse his owner. There are only a few genetic conditions recognised in the Bulldog, which will be covered in depth later in the chapter.

VACCINATION

There is much debate over the issue of vaccination at the moment. The timing of the final part of the initial vaccination course for a puppy and the frequency of subsequent booster vaccinations are both under scrutiny. An evaluation of the relative risk for each disease plays a part, depending on the local situation.

Many owners think that the actual vaccination is the protection, so that their puppy can go out for walks as soon as he or she has had the final part of the puppy vaccination course. This is not the case. The rationale behind vaccination is to stimulate the immune system into producing protective antibodies, which will be triggered if the patient is subsequently exposed to that particular disease. This means that a further one or two weeks will have to pass before an effective level of protection will have developed.

Vaccines against viruses stimulate longer-lasting protection than those against bacteria, whose effect may only persist for a matter of months in some cases. There is also the possibility of an individual failing to mount a full immune response to a vaccination: although the vaccine schedule may have been followed as recommended, that particular dog remains vulnerable.

A dog's level of protection against rabies, as demonstrated by the antibody titre in a blood sample, is routinely tested in the UK in order to fulfil the requirements of the Pet Travel Scheme (PETS). This is not required at the current time with any other individual diseases in order to gauge the need for booster vaccination or to determine the effect of a course of vaccines; instead, your veterinary surgeon will advise a protocol based upon the vaccines available, local disease prevalence, and the lifestyle of you and your dog.

It is worth remembering that

maintaining a fully effective level of immune protection against the disease appropriate to your locale is vital: these are serious diseases, which may result in the death of your dog, and some may have the potential to be passed on to his human family (so-called zoonotic potential for transmission). This is where you will be grateful for your veterinary surgeon's own knowledge and advice.

The American Animal Hospital Association laid down guidance at the end of 2006 for the vaccination of dogs in North America. Core diseases were defined as distemper, adenovirus, parvovirus and rabies. So-called non-core diseases are kennel cough, Lyme disease and leptospirosis. A decision to vaccinate against one or more non-core diseases will be based on an individual's level of risk, determined on lifestyle and where you live in the US.

Do remember, however, that the booster visit to the veterinary surgery is not 'just' for a booster. I am regularly correcting my clients when they announce that they have 'just' brought their pet for a booster. Instead, this appointment is a chance for a full health check and evaluation of how a particular dog is doing. After all, we are all conversant with the adage that a human year is equivalent to seven canine years.

There have been attempts in recent times to reset the scale for two reasons: small breeds live longer than giant breeds, and dogs are living longer than previously. I have seen dogs of 17 and 18 years of age, but to say a dog is 119 or 126 years old is plainly meaningless. It does emphasise the fact, though, that a dog's health can change dramatically over the course of a single year, because dogs age at a far faster rate than humans.

For me as a veterinary surgeon, the booster vaccination visit is a challenge: how much can I find of which the owner was unaware, such as rotten teeth or a heart murmur? Even monitoring bodyweight year upon year is of use, because bodyweight can creep up, or down, without an owner realising. Being overweight is unhealthy, but it may take an outsider's remark to make an owner realise that there is a problem. Conversely, a drop in bodyweight may be the only pointer to an underlying problem.

The diseases against which dogs are vaccinted include:

ADENOVIRUS
Canine adenovirus 1 (CAV-1) affects the liver (hepatitis) and is seen within affected dogs as the classic 'blue eye', while CAV-2 is a cause of kennel cough (see later). Vaccines often include both canine adenoviruses.

DISTEMPER
This disease is sometimes called 'hardpad' from the characteristic changes to the pads of the paws. It has a worldwide distribution, but fortunately vaccination has been very effective at reducing its occurrence. It is caused by a virus and affects the respiratory, gastro-intestinal (gut) and nervous systems, so it causes a wide range of illnesses. Fox and urban stray dog populations are most at risk and are usually responsible for local outbreaks.

KENNEL COUGH
Also known as infectious tracheobronchitis, Bordetella bronchiseptica is not only a

Find out about the incidence of disease in your locality when planning a vaccination programme.

Kennel Cough spreads rapidly among dogs that live together.

major cause of kennel cough but also a common secondary infection on top of another cause. Being a bacterium, it is susceptible to treatment with appropriate antibiotics, but the immunity stimulated by the vaccine is therefore short-lived (six to 12 months).

This vaccine is often in a form to be administered down the nostrils in order to stimulate local immunity at the point of entry, so to speak. Do not be alarmed to see your veterinary surgeon using a needle and syringe to draw up the vaccine, because the needle will be replaced with a special plastic introducer, allowing the vaccine to be gently instilled into each nostril. Dogs generally resent being held more than the actual intra-nasal vaccine, and I have learnt that covering the patient's eyes helps greatly.

Kennel cough is, however, rather a catch-all term for any cough spreading within a dog population – not just in kennels, but also between dogs at a training session or breed show, or even mixing in the park. Many of these infections may not be B. bronchiseptica but other viruses, for which one can only treat symptomatically. Parainfluenza virus is often included in a vaccine programme, as it is a common viral cause of kennel cough.

Kennel cough can seem alarming. There is a persistent cough accompanied by the production of white frothy spittle, which can last for a matter of weeks; during this time the patient is highly infectious to other dogs. I remember when it ran through our five Border Collies – there were white patches of froth on the floor wherever you looked! Other features include sneezing, a runny nose, and eyes sore with conjunctivitis. Fortunately, these infections are generally self-limiting, most dogs recovering without any long-lasting problems, but an elderly dog may be knocked sideways by it, akin to the effects of a common cold on a frail, elderly person.

LEPTOSPIROSIS

This disease is caused by *Leptospira interogans*, a spiral-shaped bacterium. There are several natural variants or serovars. Each is characteristically found in one or more particular host animal species, which then acts as a reservoir, intermittently shedding leptospires in the urine. Infection can also be picked up at mating, via bite wounds, across the placenta, or through eating the carcases of infected animals (such as rats).

A serovar will cause actual clinical disease in an individual when two conditions are fulfilled: the individual is not the natural host species, and is also not immune to that particular serovar.

Leptospirosis is a zoonotic disease, known as Weil's disease in humans, with implications for all those in contact with an affected dog. It is also commonly called rat jaundice, reflecting the rat's important role as a carrier. The UK National Rodent Survey 2003 found a wild brown rat population of 60 million, equivalent at the time to one rat per person. Wherever you live in the UK, rats are endemic, which means that there is as much a risk to the Bulldog living with a family in a town as the Bulldog leading a rural lifestyle.

Signs of illness reflect the organs affected by a particular serovar. In humans, there may be a flu-like illness or a more serious, often life-threatening disorder involving major body organs. The illness in a susceptible dog may be mild, the dog recovering within two to three weeks without treatment but going on to develop long-term liver or kidney disease. In contrast, peracute illness may result in a rapid deterioration and death following an initial malaise and fever. There may also be anorexia, vomiting, diarrhoea, abdominal pain, joint pain, increased thirst and urination rate, jaundice, and ocular changes. Haemorrhage is also a common feature, manifesting as bleeding under the skin, nosebleeds, and the presence of blood in the urine and faeces.

Treatment requires rigorous intravenous fluid therapy to support the kidneys. Being a bacterial infection, it is possible to treat leptospirosis with specific antibiotics, although a prolonged course of several weeks is needed. Strict hygiene and barrier nursing are required in order to avoid onward transmission of the disease.

Annual vaccination is recommended for leptospirosis because the immunity only lasts for a year, unlike the longer immunity associated with vaccines against viruses. There is, however, little or no cross-protection between Leptospira serovars, so vaccination will result in protection against only those serovars included in the particular vaccine used. Additionally, although vaccination against leptospirosis will prevent active disease if an individual is exposed to a serovar included in the vaccine, it cannot prevent infection of that individual and becoming a carrier in the long-term.

In the UK, vaccines have classically included *L icterohaemorrhagiae* (rat-adapted serovar) and *L canicola* (dog-specific serovar). The latter is of especial significance to us humans, since disease will not be apparent in an infected dog but leptospires will be shed intermittently.

The incidence of Lyme disease, which is transmitted by ticks, is still rare in the UK.

LYME DISEASE

This is a bacterial infection transmitted by hard ticks. It is restricted to those specific areas of the US where ticks are found, such as the north-eastern states, some southern states, California and the upper Mississippi region. It does also occur in the UK, but at a low level, so vaccination is not routinely offered.

Clinical disease is manifested primarily as limping due to arthritis, but other organs affected include the heart, kidneys and nervous system. It is readily treatable with appropriate antibiotics, once diagnosed, but the causal bacterium, Borrelia burgdorferi, is not cleared from the body totally and will persist.

Prevention requires both vaccination and tick control, especially as there are other diseases transmitted by ticks. Ticks carrying *B. Burgdorferi* will transmit it to humans as well, but an infected dog cannot pass it to a human.

PARVOVIRUS (CPV)

Canine parvovirus disease first appeared in the late 1970s, when it was feared that the UK's dog population would be decimated by it because of the lack of immunity in the general canine population. While this was a terrifying possibility at the time, fortunately it did not happen.

There are two forms of the virus (CPV-1, CPV-2) affecting domesticated dogs. It is highly contagious, picked up via the mouth/nose from infected faeces. The incubation period is about five days. CPV-2 causes two types of illness: gastro-enteritis and heart disease in puppies born to unvaccinated dams, both of which often result in death. Infection of puppies under three weeks of age with CPV-1 manifests as diarrhoea, vomiting, difficulty breathing, and fading puppy syndrome. CPV-1 can cause abortion and foetal abnormalities in breeding bitches.

Occurrence is mainly low now, thanks to vaccination, although a recent outbreak in my area did claim the lives of several dogs. It is also occasionally seen in the elderly unvaccinated dog.

Vaccination for rabies is required in many countries; in the UK, it is only needed if dogs are leaving – or returning from overseas.

website for up-to-date information – www.defra.gov.uk) then dogs can re-enter the UK without being quarantined.

Dogs to be imported into the US have to show that they were vaccinated against rabies at least 30 days previously; otherwise, they have to serve effective internal quarantine for 30 days from the date of vaccination against rabies, in order to ensure they are not incubating rabies. The exception is dogs entering from countries recognised as being rabies-free, in which case it has to be proved that they lived in that country for at least six months beforehand.

PARASITES

A parasite is defined as an organism deriving benefit on a one-way basis from another, the host. It goes without saying that it is not to the parasite's advantage to harm the host to such an extent that the benefit is lost, especially if it results in the death of the host. This means a dog could harbour parasites, internal and/or external, without there being any signs apparent to the owner. Many canine parasites can, however, transfer to humans with variable consequences, so routine preventative treatment is advised against particular parasites.

Just as with vaccination, risk assessment plays a part – for example, there is no need for routine heartworm treatment in the UK (at present), but it is vital in the US and in Mediterranean countries.

RABIES

This is another zoonotic disease and there are very strict control measures in place. Vaccines were once available in the UK only on an individual basis for dogs being taken abroad. Pets travelling into the UK had to serve six months' compulsory quarantine so that any pet incubating rabies would be identified before release back into the general population. Under the Pet Travel Scheme (PETS), provided certain criteria are met (check the DEFRA

Puppies should be routinely treated for roundworm.

ROUNDWORMS (NEMATODES)

These are the spaghetti-like worms that you may have seen passed in faeces or brought up in vomit. Most of the deworming treatments in use today cause the adult roundworms to disintegrate, thankfully, so that treating puppies in particular is not as unpleasant as it used to be!

Most puppies will have a worm burden, mainly of a particular roundworm species (Toxocara canis), which reactivates within the dam's tissues during pregnancy and passes to the foetuses developing in the womb. It is therefore important to treat the dam both during and after pregnancy, as well as the puppies.

Professional advice is to continue worming every one to three months. There are roundworm eggs in the environment and, unless you examine your dog's faeces under a microscope on a very regular basis for the presence of roundworm eggs, you will be unaware of your dog having picked up roundworms, unless he should have such a heavy burden that he passes the adults.

It takes a few weeks from the time that a dog swallows a Toxocara canis roundworm egg to himself passing viable eggs (the pre-patent period). These eggs are not immediately infective to other animals, requiring a period of maturation in the environment, which is primarily temperature-dependent and therefore shorter in the summer (as little as two weeks) than in the winter. The eggs can survive in the environment for two years and more.

There are deworming products that are active all the time, which will provide continuous protection when administered as often as directed. Otherwise, treating every month will, in effect, cut in before a dog could theoretically become a source of roundworm eggs to the general population.

It is the risk to human health that is so important: T. canis roundworms will migrate within our tissues and cause all manner of problems, not least of which (but fortunately rarely) is blindness. If a dog has roundworms, the eggs also find their way on to his coat where they can be picked up during stroking. Sensible hygiene is therefore important. You should always carefully pick up your dog's faeces and dispose of them appropriately, thereby preventing the maturation of any eggs present in the fresh faeces.

TAPEWORMS (CESTODES)

When considering the general dog population, the primary source of the commonest tapeworm species will be fleas, which can carry the eggs. Most multi-wormers will be active against these tapeworms. They are not a threat to human health, but it is unpleasant to

see the wriggly ricegrain tapeworm segments emerging from your dog's back passage while he is lying in front of the fire, and usually when you have guests for dinner!

A tapeworm of significance to human health is *Echinococcus granulosus*, found in a few parts of the UK, mainly in Wales. Man is an intermediate host for this tapeworm, along with sheep, cattle and pigs. Inadvertent ingestion of eggs passed in the faeces of an infected dog is followed by the development of

so-called hydatid cysts in major organs, such as the lungs and liver, necessitating surgical removal. Dogs become infected through eating raw meat containing hydatid cysts. Cooking will kill hydatid cysts, so avoid feeding raw meat and offal in areas of high risk.

There are specific requirements for treatment with praziquantel within 24 to 48 hours of return into the UK under the PETS. This is to prevent the inadvertent introduction of *Echinococcus*

HEARTWORM (DIROFILARIA IMMITIS)

Heartworm infection has been diagnosed in dogs all over the world. There are two prerequisites: the presence of mosquitoes, and a warm, humid climate.

When a female mosquito bites an infected animal, it acquires D. immitis in its circulating form, as microfilariae. A warm environmental temperature is needed for these microfilariae to develop into the infective third-stage larvae (L3) within the mosquitoes, the so-called intermediate host. L3 larvae are then transmitted by the mosquito when it next bites a dog. Therefore, while heartworm infection is found in all parts of the United States, it is at differing levels. An occurrence in Alaska, for example, is probably a reflection of a visiting dog having previously picked up the infection elsewhere.

Heartworm infection is not currently a problem in the UK, except for those dogs contracting it while abroad without suitable

preventative treatment. Global warming and its effect on the UK's climate, however, could change that.

It is a potentially life-threatening condition, with dogs of all breeds and ages being susceptible without preventative treatment. The larvae can grow to 14 inches within the right side of the heart, causing primarily signs of heart failure and ultimately liver and kidney damage. It can be treated but prevention is a better plan. In the US, regular blood tests for the presence of infection are advised, coupled with appropriate preventative measures, so I would advise liaison with your veterinary surgeon.

For dogs travelling to heartworm-endemic areas of the EU, such as the Mediterranean coast, preventative treatment should be started before leaving the UK and maintained during the visit. Again, this is best arranged with your veterinary surgeon.

multilocularis, a tapeworm carried by foxes on mainland Europe, which is transmissible to humans, causing serious or even fatal liver disease.

FLEAS

There are several species of flea, which are not host-specific. A dog can be carrying cat and human fleas as well as dog fleas, but the same flea treatment will kill and/or control them all. It is also accepted that environmental control is a vital part of a flea control programme. This is because the adult flea is only on the animal for as long as it takes to have a blood meal and to breed; the remainder of the life cycle occurs in the house, car, caravan, shed…

There is a vast array of flea control products available, with various routes of administration: collar, powder, spray, 'spot-on', or oral. Flea control needs to be applied to all pets in the house, regardless of whether they leave the house, since fleas can be introduced into the home by other pets and their human owners. Discuss your specific flea control needs with your veterinary surgeon.

MITES

There are five types of mite that can affect dogs.

Demodex canis: This mite is a normal inhabitant of canine hair follicles, passed from the bitch to her pups as they suckle. The development of actual skin disease or demodicosis depends

Preventative treatment is now readily available for the control of external parasites.

on the individual. It is seen frequently around the time of puberty and after a bitch's first season, associated with hormonal changes. There may, however, be an inherited weakness in an individual's immune system, enabling multiplication of the mite.

The localised form consists of areas of fur loss without itchiness, generally around the face and on the forelimbs, and 90 per cent will recover without treatment. The other 10 per cent

develop the juvenile-onset generalised form, of which half will recover spontaneously. The other half may be depressed, go off their food, and show signs of itchiness due to secondary bacterial skin infections.

Treatment is often prolonged over several months and consists of regular bathing with a specific miticidal shampoo, often clipping away fur to improve access to the skin, together with a suitable antibiotic by mouth. There is also now a licensed 'spot-on' preparation available. Progress is monitored by the examination of deep skin scrapings for the presence of the mite; the initial diagnosis is based upon abnormally high numbers of the mite, often with live individuals being seen.

Some Bulldogs may develop demodicosis for the first time in middle-age (more than four years of age). This often reflects underlying immunosuppression by an internal disease, so it is important to identify such a cause and correct it where

If your Bulldog is constantly scratching his ears and shaking his head, it could indicate the presence of ear mites.

possible, as well as treating the skin condition.

Sarcoptes scabei: This characteristically causes an intense pruritus or itchiness in the affected Bulldog, causing him to incessantly scratch and bite at himself, leading to marked fur loss and skin trauma. Initially starting on the elbows, earflaps and hocks, without treatment the skin on the rest of the body can become affected, with thickening and pigmentation of the skin. Secondary bacterial infections are common.

Unlike Demodex, this mite lives at the skin surface, and it can be hard to find in skin scrapings. It is therefore not unusual to treat a patient for sarcoptic mange (scabies) based on the appearance of the problem even with negative skin scraping findings, and especially if there is a history of contact with foxes, which are a frequent source of the scabies mite.

It will spread between dogs and can therefore also be found in situations where large numbers of dogs from different backgrounds are mixing together. It will cause itchiness in humans, although the mite cannot complete its life cycle on us, so treating all affected dogs should be sufficient. Fortunately, there is now a highly effective

'spot-on' treatment for Sarcoptes scabei.

Cheyletiella yasguri: This is the fur mite most commonly found on dogs. It is often called 'walking dandruff' because it can be possible to see collections of the small white mite moving about over the skin surface. There is excessive scale and dandruff formation, and mild itchiness. It is transmissible to humans, causing a pruritic rash.

Diagnosis is by microscopic examination of skin scrapings, coat combings and sticky tape impressions from the skin and fur. Treatment is with an appropriate insecticide, as advised by your veterinary surgeon.

Otodectes cynotis: A highly transmissible otitis externa (outer ear infection) results from the presence in the outer ear canal of this ear mite, characterised by exuberant production of dark earwax. The patient will frequently shake his head and rub at the ear(s) affected. The mites can also spread on to the skin adjacent to the opening of the external ear canal, and may transfer elsewhere, such as to the paws.

When using an otoscope to examine the outer ear canal, the heat from the light source will often cause any ear mites present to start moving around. I often offer owners the chance to have a look, because it really is quite an extraordinary sight! It is also possible to identify the mite from earwax smeared on to a slide and examined under a microscope.

Cats are a common source of ear mites. It is not unusual to find ear mites during the routine examination of puppies and kittens. Treatment options include specific eardrops acting against both the mite and any secondary infections present in the auditory canal, and certain 'spot-on' formulations. It is vital to treat all dogs and cats in the household to prevent recycling of the mite between individuals.

(Neo-) Trombicula autumnalis:
The free-living harvest mite can cause an intense local irritation on the skin. Its larvae are picked up from undergrowth, so they are characteristically found as a bright orange patch on the web of skin between the digits of the paws. It feeds on skin cells before dropping off to complete its life cycle in the environment.

Its name is a little misleading, because it is not restricted to the autumn nor to harvest-time; I find it on the earflaps of cats from late June onwards, depending on the prevailing weather. It will also bite humans.

Treatment depends on identifying and avoiding hotspots for picking up harvest mites, if possible. Checking the skin, especially the paws, after exercise and mechanically removing any mites found will reduce the chances of irritation, which can be treated symptomatically. Insecticides can

TICKS

Ticks have become an increasing problem in recent years throughout Britain. Their physical presence causes irritation, but it is their potential to spread disease that causes concern. A tick will transmit any infection previously contracted while feeding on an animal: for example Borrelia burgdorferi, the causal agent of Lyme disease (see page 132).

The life cycle of the tick is curious: each life stage takes a year to develop and move on to the next. Long grass is a major habitat. The vibration of animals moving through the grass will stimulate the larva, nymph or adult to climb up a blade of grass and wave its legs in the air as it 'quests' for a host on to which to latch for its next blood meal. Humans are as likely to be hosts, so ramblers and orienteers are advised to cover their legs when going through rough long grass.

Removing a tick is simple – provided your dog will stay still. The important rule is to twist gently so that the tick is persuaded to let go with its mouthparts. Grasp the body of the tick as near to your dog's skin as possible, either between thumb and fingers or with a specific tick-removing instrument, and then rotate in one direction until the tick comes away. I keep a plastic tick hook in my wallet at all times.

also be applied – be guided by your veterinary surgeon.

A-Z OF COMMON AILMENTS

ANAL SACS, IMPACTED
The anal sacs lie on either side of the anus at approximately four and eight o'clock, if compared with the face of a clock. They fill with a particularly pungent fluid, which is emptied on to the faeces as they move past the sacs to exit from the anus. Theories abound as to why these sacs should become impacted periodically and seemingly more so in some

dogs than others.

The irritation of impacted anal sacs is often seen as 'scooting', when the backside is dragged along the ground. Some dogs will also gnaw at their back feet or over the rump.

Increasing the fibre content of the diet helps some dogs; in others, there is underlying skin disease. It may be a one-off occurrence for no apparent reason. Sometimes an infection can become established, requiring antibiotic therapy, which may need to be coupled with flushing out the infected sac under sedation or general anaesthesia. More rarely, a dog will present with an apparently acute-onset anal sac abscess, which is incredibly painful.

DIARRHOEA
Cause and treatment much as Gastritis (see below).

EAR INFECTIONS
The dog has a long external ear canal, initially vertical then horizontal, leading to the eardrum, which protects the middle ear. If your Bulldog is shaking his head, then his ears will need to be inspected with an auroscope by a veterinary surgeon in order to identify any cause, and to ensure the eardrum is intact. A sample may be taken from the canal to be examined under the microscope and cultured, to identify causal agents before prescribing appropriate eardrops containing antibiotic, antifungal agent and/or steroid. Predisposing causes of otitis externa or infection in the external ear canal include:
• Presence of a foreign body, such as a grass awn
• Ear mites, which are intensely irritating to the dog and stimulate the production of brown wax, predisposing to infection
• Previous infections, causing

Routine checking and grooming will ensure you spot any health problems at an early stage.

the canal's lining to thicken, narrowing the canal and reducing ventilation
• Swimming – some Bulldogs will swim, but water trapped in the external ear canal can lead to infection, especially if the water is not clean.

FOREIGN BODIES
• **Internal:** Items swallowed in haste without checking whether they will be digested can cause problems if they lodge in the stomach or

obstruct the intestines, necessitating surgical removal. Acute vomiting is the main indication. Common objects I have seen removed include stones from the garden, peach stones, babies' dummies, golf balls, and, once, a lady's bra…

It is possible to diagnose a dog with an intestinal obstruction across a waiting room from a particularly 'tucked-up' stance and pained facial expression. These patients bounce back from surgery dramatically. A previously docile and compliant obstructed patient will return for a post-operative check-up and literally bounce into the consulting room.
• **External:** Grass awns are adept at finding their way into orifices such as a nostril, down an ear, and into the soft skin between two digits (toes), whence they start a one-way journey due to the direction of their whiskers. In particular, I remember a grass awn that migrated from a hindpaw, causing abscesses along the way but not yielding itself up until it erupted through the skin in the groin!

It is inevitable that your Bulldog will scavenge from time to time, and this may result in gastric upset.

GASTRITIS

This is usually a simple stomach upset, most commonly in response to dietary indiscretion. Scavenging constitutes a change in the diet as much as an abrupt switch in the food being fed by the owner.

There are also some specific infections causing more severe gastritis/enteritis, which will require treatment from a veterinary surgeon (see also Canine Parvovirus under 'Vaccination' on page 133).

Generally, a day without food, followed by a few days of small, frequent meals of a bland diet (such as cooked chicken or fish), or an appropriate prescription diet, should allow the stomach to settle. It is vital to ensure the patient is drinking and retaining sufficient water to cover losses resulting from the stomach upset in addition to the normal losses to be expected when healthy. Oral rehydration fluid may not be very appetising for the patient, in which case cooled boiled water should be offered. Fluids should initially be offered in small but frequent amounts to avoid over-drinking, which can result in further vomiting and thereby dehydration and electrolyte imbalances. It is also important to wean the patient back on to routine food gradually or else another bout of gastritis may occur.

JOINT PROBLEMS

It is not unusual for older Bulldogs to be stiff after exercise, particularly in cold weather. Your veterinary surgeon will be able to advise you on ways of helping your dog cope with stiffness, not least of which will be to ensure that he is not overweight. Arthritic joints do not need to be burdened with extra bodyweight!

LUMPS & BUMPS

Regularly handling and stroking your dog will enable the early detection of lumps and bumps. These may be due to infection (abscess), bruising, multiplication of particular cells from within the body, or even an external parasite (tick). If you are worried about any lump you find, have it checked by a veterinary surgeon.

Gnawing on a marrow bone will help to promote dental health.

OBESITY

Being overweight does predispose to many other problems, such as diabetes mellitus, heart disease and joint problems. It is so easily prevented by simply acting as your Bulldog's conscience. Ignore pleading eyes and feed according to your dog's waistline. The body condition is what matters qualitatively, alongside monitoring that individual's bodyweight as a quantitative measure. The Bulldog should, in my opinion as a health professional, have at least a suggestion of a waist and it should be possible to feel the ribs beneath only a slight layer of fat.

Neutering does not automatically mean that your Bulldog will be overweight. Having an ovario-hysterectomy does slow down the body's rate of working, castration to a lesser extent, but it therefore means that your dog needs less food. I recommend cutting back a little on the amount of food fed a few weeks before neutering to accustom your Bulldog to less food. If she looks a little underweight on the morning of the operation, it will help the veterinary surgeon as well as giving her a little leeway weight-wise afterwards. It is always harder to lose weight after neutering than before, because of this slowing in the body's inherent metabolic rate.

TEETH PROBLEMS

Eating food starts with the canine teeth gripping and killing prey in the wild, incisor teeth biting off pieces of food and the molar teeth chewing it. To be able to eat is vital for life, yet the actual health of the teeth is often overlooked: unhealthy teeth can predispose to disease, and not just by reducing the ability to eat. The presence of infection within the mouth can lead to bacteria entering the bloodstream and then filtering out at major organs, with the potential for serious consequences. That is not to forget that simply having dental pain can affect a dog's wellbeing, as anyone who has had toothache will confirm.

Responsible breeders work tirelessly to ensure their breeding stock are free from inherited diseases.

Veterinary dentistry has made huge leaps in recent years, so that it no longer consists of extraction as the treatment of necessity. Good dental health lies in the hands of the owner, starting from the moment the dog comes into your care. Just as we have taken on responsibility for feeding, so we have acquired the task of maintaining good dental and oral hygiene. In an ideal world, we should brush our dogs' teeth as regularly as our own, but the Bulldog puppy who finds having his teeth brushed is a huge game and excuse to roll over and over on the ground requires loads of patience, twice a day.

There are alternative strategies, ranging from dental chewsticks to specially formulated foods, but the main thing is to be aware of your dog's mouth. At least train your puppy to permit full examination of his teeth. This will not only ensure you are checking in his mouth regularly but will also make your veterinary surgeon's job easier when there is a real need for your dog to 'open wide!'

INHERITED DISORDERS

Any individual, dog or human, may have an inherited disorder by virtue of the genes acquired from the parents. This is significant not only for the health of that individual but also because of the potential for transmitting the disorder on to that individual's offspring and to subsequent generations, depending on the mode of inheritance.

There are control schemes in place for some inherited disorders. In the US, for example, the Canine Eye Registration Foundation (CERF) was set up by dog breeders concerned about heritable eye disease, and provides a database of dogs who have been examined by diplomates of the American College of Veterinary Ophthalmologists.

To date, only a few conditions have been confirmed in the Bulldog as being hereditary. In alphabetical order, these include:

The Bulldog owner must provide a constant supply of cool, fresh water in hot weather.

BRACHYCEPHALIC AIRWAY OBSTRUCTION SYNDROME

This is a major problem arising from a variety of anatomical defects, such as an elongated soft palate, narrowed nostrils, abnormalities in the larynx and/or relatively small windpipe (hypoplastic trachea), as well as the relatively short head of the Bulldog (hence 'brachycephalic'). The effects on breathing range widely from snuffling and snorting to difficulty breathing, a reduced ability to exercise and, in severe cases, collapse. Sedation and general anaesthesia require extreme caution.

Hot weather, excitement and stress will increase respiratory distress. I particularly remember being called out to a Bulldog who had collapsed in a car while travelling on a hot summer's day. We had to admit him for an emergency tracheotomy to enable him to breathe more easily and effectively.

The usual defences to guard the airways when swallowing food may be affected because of the difficulty in breathing. Vomiting and gagging from swallowing air, and aspiration pneumonia from inhaling food matter or saliva are not uncommon. I have also treated gastric dilatation in a Bulldog.

CONGENITAL DEAFNESS

This appears to be linked to the piebald gene, with deafness resulting from degeneration of part of the blood supply to the cochlea during the first few weeks of life. It is now possible to accurately assess a puppy's hearing from the age of five weeks using the Brainstem Auditory Evoked Response Test, which is painless.

CRYPTORCHIDISM

During foetal development, the testicles form high within the abdomen and migrate down through the abdomen, out along the inguinal canal and into their final position in the scrotum. A dog is said to be cryptorchid if one or both testicles is absent from the scrotum and is instead located within the inguinal canal or within the abdomen. In the Bulldog, this is thought to be inherited in a sex-limited, autosomal recessive fashion.

ELBOW DYSPLASIA

A juvenile Bulldog with a swollen and painful elbow, resulting in lameness, may have elbow dysplasia due to an ununited anconeal process. This can be diagnosed with radiographs taken of the elbow.

Another elbow condition reported in the Bulldog is

congenital luxation. This characteristically becomes apparent in the four- or five-month-old Bulldog.

ENTROPION

This is an inrolling of the eyelids, usually of the lower eyelid when it occurs in the Bulldog. There are degrees of entropion, ranging from a slight inrolling to the more serious case requiring surgical correction because of the pain and damage to the surface of the eyeball.

HAEMOPHILIA A

Haemophilia is the most common of the blood coagulation disorders in humans and animals, inherited in a sex-linked recessive fashion. This means that the male is either affected or clear, while females can alternatively be carriers for the trait. Haemophilia A arises from a deficiency of blood-clotting Factor VIII.

There are many ways in which haemophilia A can manifest, at worst as sudden death. There may be early indications, such as prolonged bleeding when the baby teeth are lost or unexpected bruising under the skin. A problem may not become apparent until after surgery, such as routine neutering or an injury. Treatment will often require a blood transfusion.

HEMIVERTEBRAE

The vertebrae are the building blocks of the bony spine, designed to protect the spinal cord as it runs from the underside of the brain, down the length of the back through the canal enclosed within them. In the Bulldog, hemivertebrae are misshapen, wedge-shaped deformed thoracic vertebrae whose protective role is therefore compromised. Effects on the individual will be determined by the nature of the deformity, with kyphosis or kinking of the vertebral column, spinal cord compression, hindlimb weakness and pain, and, at worst, resulting in paralysis. Surgery may be possible but needs careful pre-operative evaluation.

HIP DYSPLASIA

Malformation of the hip joints results in pain, lameness and reduced exercise tolerance in the

Hip joints can be X-rayed and scored, and this is an important factor when selecting dogs that might be suitable for breeding.

young dog with hip dysplasia, and resulting in degenerative joint disease (arthritis) in the older dog. Each hip joint is scored on several features to give a total of zero to 53 from a radiograph taken with the hips and pelvis in a specified position, usually requiring the dog to be sedated, after the age of one year under the BVA/KC* Scheme, from two years of age in the US (OFA**).

Just 18 individual Bulldogs had been screened under the BVA/KC Scheme by 1 November 2007, giving a mean summated score for both hips of 43 but range of 10-96. Hip dysplasia is perceived as a major problem in the breed in the US.

KERATOCONJUNCTIVITIS SICCA (KCS, DRY EYE)

Each eye is lubricated by tears produced by two tear glands, one within the eye socket and another smaller one associated with the third eyelid. There appears to be a breed predisposition for KCS, which results when there is inadequate tear production by the glands (hence 'dry eye'), and is usually bilateral, affecting the tear glands in both eyes. It is characterised by a sore red appearance to the eye with a thick ocular discharge and, ultimately, clouding of the cornea and loss of vision. The cause is generally unknown or inherited but, rarely, dry eye may result from trauma, infection, hypothyroidism or an

adverse reaction to a drug.

Diagnosis is made with a Schirmer tear strip, which assesses the tear production in each eye. Surgical transposition of the parotid salivary duct was the favoured treatment, but medical therapy is now more often the therapy of choice, aimed at stimulating the underactive tear glands.

MITRAL VALVE DYSPLASIA (MVD)

This is a congenital heart defect: an affected individual is born with a malformed heart valve between the two chambers of the left side of the heart. The heart's ability to act as a pump depends on the integrity of its valves. A

Mitral valve dysplasia can be detected when a puppy has his first health check.

wide spectrum of effect is seen, ranging from a slight malformation, having little effect on life span, across to such a leaky valve that congestive heart failure develops whilst young.

Blood leaking back through the valve causes turbulence in the blood flow, and the normally clear click as the valve closes is muffled. This is heard as a murmur when a stethoscope is placed on the chest wall, especially over the valve, so that a common time to first suspect MVD is when a veterinary surgeon examines the puppy as a first health check or prior to starting a vaccination course. A detailed ultrasound examination is needed to diagnose and assess the extent of the problem.

UROLITHIASIS

This is the presence of stones or excessive amounts of crystals within the urinary tract, most commonly in the bladder. They irritate the lining of the urinary tract, resulting in pain and blood in the urine. They may predispose to a secondary bacterial infection. In some instances, they may actually partially or totally block the outflow of urine, which requires emergency treatment.

Different biochemical types of uroliths have been recognised. Some surveys of the Bulldog have found a higher than expected incidence of cystine and urate uroliths, with a possible predisposition in male Bulldogs. A new KC/BVA DNA test is now available.

PATELLAR LUXATION

This is the condition that I point out to my children when I spot a dog walking along the road, giving a little hop for a few steps every now and again. The kneecap or patella is slipping out of position, locking the knee or stifle so that it will not bend, and causing the characteristic hopping steps until the patella slips back into its position over the stifle joint.

Surgical correction is possible in severely affected dogs, but many simply carry on intermittently hopping, the long-term effect being inevitably arthritis of the stifle.

*British Veterinary Association/Kennel Club
**Orthopedic Foundation for Animals

COMPLEMENTARY THERAPIES

Just as for human health, I do believe that there is a place for alternative therapies alongside and complementing orthodox treatment under the supervision of a veterinary surgeon. That is why 'complementary therapies' is a better name.

Because animals do not have a choice, there are measures in place to safeguard their wellbeing and welfare. All manipulative treatment must be under the direction of a veterinary surgeon who has examined the patient and diagnosed the condition that he or she feels needs that form of treatment. This covers physiotherapy, chiropractic, osteopathy and swimming therapy. For example, dogs with arthritis who cannot exercise as freely as they were accustomed will enjoy the sensation of controlled non-weight-bearing exercise in water, and will benefit with improved muscling and overall fitness.

All other complementary therapies such as acupuncture, homoeopathy and aromatherapy, can only be carried out by veterinary surgeons who have been trained in that particular field. Acupuncture is mainly used in dogs for pain relief, often to good effect. The needles look more alarming to the owner, but they are very fine and are well tolerated by most canine patients. Speaking personally, superficial needling is not unpleasant and does help with pain relief.

Increasingly owners are becoming aware of the benefit of complementary therapies.

Homoeopathy has had a mixed press in recent years. It is based on the concept of treating like with like. Additionally, a homoeopathic remedy is said to become more powerful the more it is diluted.

CONCLUSION

As the owner of a Bulldog, you are responsible for his care and health. Not only must you make decisions on his behalf, you are also responsible for establishing a lifestyle for him that will ensure he leads a long and happy life. Diet plays an important part in this, as does exercise.

For the domestic dog, it is only in recent years that the need has been recognised for changing the diet to suit the dog as he grows, matures and then enters his twilight years. So-called life-stage diets try to match the nutritional needs of the dog as he progresses through life.

An adult dog food will suit the Bulldog living a standard family life. There are also foods for those Bulldogs tactfully termed as obese-prone, such as those who have been neutered or are less active than others, or simply like their food. Do remember, though, that ultimately you are in control of your Bulldog's diet, unless he is able to profit from scavenging!

On the other hand, prescription diets are of necessity fed under the supervision of a veterinary surgeon because each is formulated to meet the very specific needs of particular health conditions. Should a prescription diet be fed to a healthy dog, or to a dog with a different illness, there could be adverse effects.

It is important to remember that your Bulldog has no choice. As his owner, you are responsible for any decision made, so it must be as informed a decision as possible. Always speak to your vet if you have any worries about your Bully. He is not just a dog; from the moment you brought him home, he became a member of the family.

The Bulldog is not the easiest breed to care for, but with good care and management, your dog will enjoy an active, happy and healthy life.

THE CONTRIBUTORS

THE EDITOR:
MALCOLM PRESLAND
(KOFYN)

Malcolm was brought up with Standard Bull Terriers and Boxers and after he left home kept Boxers, which he bred but only lightly exhibited. He bought his first Bulldog, Uachter Taleen, in 1983 but work commitments prevented serious campaigning. In the early 1990s he founded the Kofyn kennel with his wife, Melanie. They soon made up their first Bulldog, Ch. & Irish Ch. Macracken Golden Rain In Kofyn, who was also the first post-war dual Anglo/Irish Champion bitch. Her progeny included Ch. & Ned. Ch. Kofyn Kasts the Runes (also a UK RCC winner), Kofyn Kwite Outrageous For Macracken CC/BIS winner, Kofyn Klearly Conspicous RCC winner, and the famous Kofyn Kawtcha Lookin – sire of Champions in the UK and Europe. Other RCC winners they have bred or owned include Kofyn Krypt Keeper, Kofyn Kwiot Riot At Kikuchi, Kofyn Kamera Lites Action, Kofyn Kuminatcha and Kikuchi Kendera In Kofyn. Kofyn Karlsberg Export is a CACIB & CAC winner in Europe.

Malcolm awards CCs in Bulldogs in the UK and has judged them in Europe several times and in America three times. He is the Bulldog breed corespondent for Our Dogs weekly dog magazine and was secretary of the Junior Bulldog Club for several years. He is currently the press officer for the Bulldog Breed Council, he is also a member of the Kennel Club. In addition to Bulldogs, Malcolm's other love is the Miniature Bull Terrier several of which live with the Bulldogs as part of the Kofyn Show Team.
See Chapter One: Getting To Know the Bulldog and Chapter Seven: The Perfect Bulldog.

TONY DARMANIN (SUTUS)

Tony was introduced to the word of Bulldogs by his wife, Barbara, who grew up with the breed. In fact, her father owned his first Bulldog in 1925 when he was just 13 years old. He bred Barbara and Tony's first Bulldog, Earl Benjamin, who won at Championship Show level, as well as obtaining his stud book entry. Next, they bought a young, brindle bitch, Leebarton Isis, and bred their first litter. They joined several Bulldog clubs and became committee members of the Birmingham and Midland Counties Bulldog Club, where Tony served as secretary in the early 1980s. Later, Tony served on the committee of the Bulldog Club Incorporated, started stewarding and then judging in the UK. In the 1980s, Tony and Barbara went to live in the USA, together with 10 Bulldogs, and got involved in the Bulldog scene, joining local Bulldog clubs and showing their dogs. In 1992, they returned to the UK and were voted on to the committee of the 'Birmingham' where Tony served as the club's secretary from 1998 to 2010. He first awarded CC's in the breed in1994 and in 2000, and following early retirement has judged the breed at

CC level in Australia, Bulgaria, the Czech Republic, Denmark. France, Holland, Hungary, Spain, Switzerland and the USA. He chaired the Bulldog Breed Council Education sub committee from 2007-2010.
See Chapter Two: The First Bulldogs.

PETER DAVIES (KISMOND)

Originally qualified as a biologist, Peter recently took planned retirement from the post of Chief Operating Officer of the Barts and The London, Queen Mary's School of Medicine & Dentistry, University of London, where he had worked for seven years. After working in the NHS and University sector for 42 years, he is now enjoying spending more time at home with his family and dogs.

His main outside interest for over 40 years, shared with his wife Sandra, has been the breeding and exhibiting of dogs at Open and Championship Shows. They originally had boxers, gaining considerable success during the 1970s and 1980s. Their affix, Kismond, was first registered with the Kennel Club in 1975.

However, Peter and Sandra always wanted a Bulldog and purchased their first one in 1998. Since that time they have concentrated on Bulldogs and have achieved considerable success for a small hobby kennel. Their first Bulldog, Ch Shiloh Patchwork at Kismond JW, was not only successfully campaigned to her title but also to the ultimate accolade of Bulldog of the Year in 2002. Since then they have campaigned a further eight dogs, either home bred or sired by one of their stud dogs and six of these have achieved a stud book number including the well known Kismond Buttons 'N' Bows JW, ShCM who won 2 CCs and 4 RCCs. They are at present the only Bulldog kennel to have qualified a Bulldog for the final of the PetPlan Junior Stakes, were the first kennel in England to qualify a bulldog for the ShCM award and the first to campaign a full brother and sister to their JW title.

Peter has been a committee member of the Bath & Western Counties Bulldog Club for over 10 years and has served as the Chairman and Treasurer for the past six years.
See Chapter Three: A Bulldog For Your Lifestyle.

TANIA HOLMES (SHALONEY)

Tania got her first Bulldog when she met her husband in 1991. Since then they have owned a total of 13 Bulldogs, 4 of which are still living at home with them.

She bred her first litter in July 1999 under the Shaloney affix and showed fairly successfully until 2001 when she and her husband took over the UK Bulldog Rescue, which became a registered charity in 2006. Tania has to date rehomed more than 1000 bulldogs.

Tania holds an Advance breeding certificate, a Dog Breeding Diploma, a Rehoming certificate, is canine first aid trained and is an Accredited Pet

Care Professional. She is currently also studying to become an SQP via AMTRA.

Having written one book already, Tania has almost 20 years experience with a breed she has dedicated her life to, giving up her home and most of her garden to Bulldog Rescue which can be contacted via www.bulldogrescue.co.uk
See Chapter Four: The New Arrival.

MELANIE VINCENT-PRESLAND (KOFYN)

Melanie grew up in a show dog home as her mother, Ann, showed Poodles and Borzoi; Melanie first went into the show ring with a Borzoi. During the early 1980s she handled Great Danes for a friend, but at that time her first love was obedience and the 'new' sport of dog agility. While attending Paignton Championship show in 1984, she met and fell in love with the Akita which had just arrived in the UK and became completely hooked on the both the breed and dog showing. In 1991 she began taking her friends' two Bulldogs to shows along with her Akitas, and this is where the Bulldog love affair began. In 1992 Melanie met Malcolm Presland and they joined forces under the Kofyn affix with Bulldogs, Akitas, and the odd Chihuahua – but the Bulldogs soon took over!

Melanie has competed in obedience with the Bulldog, Kofyn Klearly Conspicuous, and also likes to train her Bulldogs to take part in fun agility and gundog scurries. She has judged Bulldogs at Championship show level in the UK, on the Continent and in America. Melanie served several years as treasurer for a Bulldog club and is a member of the Kennel Club.
See Chapter Five: The Best of Care.

JULIA BARNES

Julia has owned and trained a number of different dog breeds, and has also worked as a puppy socialiser for Dogs for the Disabled. A former journalist, she has written many books, including several on dog training and behaviour. Julia is indebted to Melanie Vincent-Presland for her specialist knowledge about training Bulldogs.
See Chapter Six: Training and Socialisation.

ALISON LOGAN MA VetMB MRCVS

Alison qualified as a veterinary surgeon from Cambridge University in 1989, having been brought up surrounded by all manner of animals and birds in the north Essex countryside. She has been in practice in her home town ever since, living with her husband, two children and Labrador Retriever Pippin.

She contributes on a regular basis to *Veterinary Times, Veterinary Nurse Times, Dogs Today, Cat World* and *Pet Patter*, the PetPlan newsletter. In 1995, Alison won the Univet Literary Award with an article on Cushing's Disease, and she won it again (as the Vetoquinol Literary Award) in 2002, writing about common conditions in the Shar-Pei.
See Chapter Eight: Happy and Healthy.

USEFUL ADDRESSES

BREED CLUBS

To obtain up-to-date contact information for the following breed clubs, please contact the Kennel Club:

- Bath and Western Counties Bulldog Club
- Birmingham and Midland counties Bulldog Club
- Blackpool and Fylde Bulldog Club
- British Bulldog Club
- Bulldog Breed Council
- Bulldog Club (Incorporated)
- Bulldog Club of Scotland
- Bulldog Club of Wales
- Bulldog Rescue
- East Midland Bulldog Club
- Junior Bulldog Club
- London Bulldog Society
- Manchester and Counties Bulldog Club
- Northern Bulldog Club
- Northumberland and Durham Bulldog Club
- Plymouth, Devon and Cornwall Bulldog Club
- Rochdale and District Bulldog Club
- Sheffield and Leodensian Bulldog Club
- South of England Bulldog Society
- Yorkshire Bulldog Club.

KENNEL CLUBS

American Kennel Club (AKC)
5580 Centerview Drive
Raleigh, NC 27606
Telephone: 919 233 9767
Fax: 919 233 3627
Email: info@akc.org
Web: www.akc.org

The Kennel Club (UK)
1 Clarges Street London, W1J 8AB
Telephone: 0870 606 6750
Fax: 0207 518 1058
Web: www.the-kennel-club.org.uk

TRAINING AND BEHAVIOUR

Association of Pet Dog Trainers
PO Box 17, Kempsford, GL7 4WZ
Telephone: 01285 810811
Email: APDToffice@aol.com
Web: http://www.apdt.co.uk

Association of Pet Behaviour Counsellors
PO BOX 46, Worcester, WR8 9YS
Telephone: 01386 751151

Fax: 01386 750743
Email: info@apbc.org.uk
Web: http://www.apbc.org.uk/

ACTIVITIES

Agility Club
http://www.agilityclub.co.uk/

British Flyball Association
PO Box 990, Doncaster, DN1 9FY
Telephone: 01628 829623
Email: secretary@flyball.org.uk
Web: http://www.flyball.org.uk/

World Canine Freestyle Organisation
P.O. Box 350122, Brooklyn, NY 11235-2525, USA
Telephone: (718) 332-8336
Fax: (718) 646-2686
Email: wcfodogs@aol.com
Web: www.worldcaninefreestyle.org

HEALTH

Alternative Veterinary Medicine Centre, Chinham House, Stanford in the Vale, Oxfordshire, SN7 8NQ
Telephone: 01367 710324
Fax: 01367 718243
Web: www.alternativevet.org/

Animal Health Trust
Lanwades Park, Kentford, Newmarket, Suffolk, CB8 7UU
Telephone: 01638 751000
Web: www.aht.org.uk

British Association of Veterinary Ophthalmologists (BAVO)
Email: secretary@bravo.org.uk
Web: http://www.bravo.org.uk/

British Small Animal Veterinary Association
Woodrow House, 1 Telford Way, Waterwells Business Park, Quedgeley, Gloucestershire, GL2 2AB
Telephone: 01452 726700
Fax: 01452 726701
Email: customerservices@bsava.com
Web: http://www.bsava.com/

British Veterinary Hospitals Association
Station Bungalow, Main Rd, Stocksfield, Northumberland, NE43 7HJ

Telephone: 07966 901619
Fax: 07813 915954
Email: office@bvha.org.uk
Web: http://www.bvha.org.uk/

Royal College of Veterinary Surgeons
Belgravia House, 62-64 Horseferry Road, London, SW1P 2AF
Telephone: 0207 222 2001
Fax: 0207 222 2004
Email: admin@rcvs.org.uk
Web: www.rcvs.org.uk

ASSISTANCE DOGS

Canine Partners
Mill Lane, Heyshott, Midhurst, West Sussex, GU29 0ED
Telephone: 08456 580480
Fax: 08456 580481
Web: www.caninepartners.co.uk

Dogs for the Disabled
The Frances Hay Centre, Blacklocks Hill, Banbury, Oxon, OX17 2BS
Telephone: 01295 252600
Web: www.dogsforthedisabled.org

Guide Dogs for the Blind Association
Burghfield Common, Reading, RG7 3YG
Telephone: 01189 835555
Fax: 01189 835433
Web: www.guidedogs.org.uk/

Hearing Dogs for Deaf People
The Grange, Wycombe Road, Saunderton, Princes Risborough, Bucks, HP27 9NS
Telephone: 01844 348100
Fax: 01844 348101
Web: www.hearingdogs.org.uk

Pets as Therapy
3a Grange Farm Cottages, Wycombe Road, Saunderton, Princes Risborough, Bucks, HP27 9NS
Telephone: 01845 345445
Fax: 01845 550236
Web: http://www.petsastherapy.org/

Support Dogs
21 Jessops Riverside, Brightside Lane, Sheffield, S9 2RX
Tel: 01142 617800
Fax: 01142 617555
Email: supportdogs@btconnect.com
Web: www.support-dogs.org.uk

Help us turn paws into helping hands

Sponsor a **Dogs for the Disabled** puppy for just £5.00 per month and you could help change someone's life.

www.dogsforthedisabled.org   Telephone: 01295 252600

Dogs for the Disabled

Registered charity number: 1092960